DIANA SCOTT was born in Massachusetts in 1947, and spent her childhood and adolescence in London where she was introduced to 'pacifism, democracy, the Campaign for Nuclear Disarmament, Shakespeare, opera, literature and academic achievement'. In 1968 she took a Bachelor of Arts degree in Drama and Theatre Arts and Greek at Birmingham University. She then began to teach English as a second language and to write poetry, which has since been widely published in magazines and anthologies. In the early seventies she became involved in the women's movement, and joined a women's poetry performance group, Prodigal Daughters, giving readings and combining poetry with dance, music and drama. In 1977 she and her co-author, Mary Coghill, published *If women want to speak, what language do they use?* In recent years she has 'written a lot of poetry, read a lot of poetry books, started to make a lot of jokes, even some money, and run a thousand miles'. Diana Scott now lives in Leeds where she works as a poet, writer, teacher and mother.

Bread and Roses grew out of Diana Scott's interest in the nature of inspiration and the creative process in women's writing. Rich and wide-ranging in its selection of British, American and European poetry from the 1820s to the present day, and including famous and lesser known writers, the approach is one of depth rather than breadth, giving each poet the space to express her range. Diana Scott's illuminating and affectionate introductions, telling of the poets' lives, of their shared visions and symbols, their struggles as women and poets, do much to make this an absorbing and inspiring collection.

'Bread and Roses' was a slogan of a historic women textile workers' strike, a landmark of the early American labour movement; strike and slogan were later commemorated in a song still popular today. As the song has it, 'yes, it is Bread we fight for, but we fight for Roses too'.

If you would like to know more about Virago books, write to us at Ely House, 37 Dover Street, London W1X 4HS for a full catalogue.

Please send a stamped addressed envelope

Bread and Roses

AN ANTHOLOGY OF NINETEENTH- AND TWENTIETH-CENTURY POETRY BY WOMEN WRITERS

Compiled and introduced by
DIANA SCOTT

Virago

Published by VIRAGO PRESS Limited 1982
Ely House, 37 Dover Street, London W1X 4HS

Set in IBM 11 point Baskerville by Tek Art, Croydon, Surrey and printed in Finland by Werner Söderström Oy, a member of Finnprint

British Library Cataloguing in Publication Data
Bread and roses: an anthology of nineteenth and
twentieth-century poetry by women writers.
1. English poetry – Women authors
I. Scott, Diana
821'.008'09287 PR1178.W6

ISBN 0-86068-235-8

FOR KATIE AND JOHN HARRIS

CONTENTS

NOTE

As well as having page references, the poems are numbered consecutively. When a poem is quoted in an introduction, it is also given its number, for easy reference.

Acknowledgements

For permission to publish or reproduce the poems in this book grateful acknowledgement is made to the following:

For the poems of Frances Cornford and Stevie Smith, to their respective executors Christopher Cornford and James MacGibbon; to Frances Cornford's publishers Hutchinson and to Allen Lane who publish *The Collected Poems of Stevie Smith.*

For the poems of Charlotte Mew to Carcanet Press and Virago Press.

'March of the Women' by Cicely Hamilton is printed by permission of J. Curwen & Sons Ltd., London.

In the case of copyright material, to the authors of the poems.

To all the authors anyway, for writing their poems.

Every effort has been made to trace copyright holders of material in this book.

The editor and publishers apologise if any material has been included without permission and would be glad to hear from anyone who has not been consulted.

This book has been supported by financial assistance from the Leonard Cohen Educational Trust and Yorkshire Arts Association.

The editor gratefully acknowledges the assistance of the staffs of the Language and Literature Collection, Manchester Public Libraries, the Brotherton Library, University of Leeds, and the Museum of London Library for help in obtaining research materials; and the support of Ursula Owen at Virago Press.

Some of this material has appeared elsewhere. The poems by Charlotte Mew are included in *Collected Poems and Prose of Charlotte Mew* published by Carcanet Press and Virago. The poems of Stevie Smith are published in *Collected Poems of Stevie Smith* published by Allen Lane. The poem 'From an Asylum' comes from *Correspondences,* published by Oxford University Press. The poem 'Expectant Mother' comes from *The Orchard Upstairs,* published by Oxford University Press and reproduced with permission. Of Nicki Jackowska's poems, 'Family Outing' was first published in *Ambit,* the 'Insect Kitchen' in *Bananas.* The song by Frankie Armstrong, 'Women of My Land', appears in *Stand Together: A New Songbook,* published by Hackney and Islington Music Workshop. The poems 'To Our Daughter' by Jennifer Armitage, 'My Son and I' and 'Cabbage' by Rosemary Norman, 'Houseplant' by Felicity Napier and 'Why So Many of Them Die' by Susan Wallbank appear in *Houseplant,* a pamphlet produced by the authors and others. 'The Succubus' by Harriet Rose appeared in *Word 10.* 'Lucy Taking Birth' by Diana Scott appeared in *P.E.N. Anthology 1976/77,* published by

Hutchinson. Astra's 'Daughters' appeared in *Seven Women*, published by the Women's Literature Collective. The poem 'Mothers of Sons' by Lesley Saunders appears in the author's collection 'The Cradle and the Grave'. Fran Winant's work is published by Violet Press, New York. Work by Jo Barnes and Maureen Burge and many other worker writers is published by Bristol Broadsides. Asphodel's poems have been published by the Women's Poetry Publishing Collective. 'In Memory, 1978' by Judith Kazantzis first appeared in *Spare Rib* and appears in *The Wicked Queen*, published by Sidgwick and Jackson. Her three other poems, 'Arachne', 'The Frightened Flier Goes North', 'A Woman Making Advances Publicly' appear in *Touch Papers*, by Judith Kazantzis, Michele Roberts and Michelene Wandor, published by Allison and Busby. 'The Rime of the Ancient Feminist' by Stephanie Markman is published in full by Stramullion Press. 'Magnificat' and 'Madwoman at Rodmell' appear in *Touch Papers*.

Permission to reprint or broadcast copyright material in this anthology must be obtained from Virago Press, Ely House, 37 Dover Street, London W1X 4HS and from the individual poet with whom the copyright rests. The usual acknowledgement must be made to the publishers. In case of difficulty, the editor is willing to forward letters to contributors. She may be contacted through the publishers. The National Poetry Secretariat, 21 Earls Court Square, London SW5, and the London Poetry Secretariat, 25/31 Tavistock Place, London WC1 9SG, are able to assist individuals who wish to contact poets in connection with poetry readings, publication, etc., as they did me.

Introduction

ON READING POETRY

In this book I have created a sequence of poems that begins in the 1820s and continues up to the present day. My purpose was to create a collection that would give pleasure both to readers who have not read much poetry, and to those who feel that poetry is already very much part of their lives. As a poet, I believe that the experience of creating poetry is valuable, exciting, and worthy of attention.

Artists, scientists, religious mystics, and others, have documented what we may call inspiration in much the same terms as poets and it seems that 'inspiration' may be an experience accessible to people in all walks of life.

Thought followed thought – star followed star
Through boundless regions on
While one sweet influence, near and far,
Thrilled through and proved us one.

Why did the morning rise to break
So great, so pure a spell,
And scorch with fire the tranquil cheek
Where your cool radiance fell?

Emily Brontë (6)

Some poetry communicates the experience with perfect clarity. It may empower us to recreate the experience for ourselves. Some poetry maps the experience of inspiration in precise detail. Decoded – for what is being communicated may not be instantly clear – it gives full directions as to how to get to it.

The poetry in this collection is divided into four sections: two nineteenth- and two twentieth-century sections. In those sections will be found introductory remarks and biographical notes that relate specifically to these sections. My purpose in this general introduction is to create a definition of inspiration, in simple terms, that may support the reader. It is also to suggest some straightforward ways of approaching the poems.

The introductions that follow now are intended chiefly for the reader newish to poetry. You may wish to read them now, or to refer to them while you are reading the poetry, or to read them after you have read the poetry, or not to read them at all. They are there to be used, just like the poetry, by the reader, and in the reader's own way.

TOWARDS A DEFINITION OF INSPIRATION

> My imagination, unbidden, possessed and guided me, gifting the successive images that arose in my mind with a vividness far beyond the usual bounds of reveries. I saw – with shut eyes, but with acute mental vision – I saw the pale student of unhallowed arts . . . I saw the hideous phantasm of a man stretched out . . .
>
> (Mary Shelley)

> Like to write? Of course, of course I do. I seem to live while I write – it is life for me. Why what is to live? Not to eat and drink and breathe, but to feel the life in you down all the fibres of being, passionately and joyfully. And thus one lives in composition surely – not always – but when the wheel goes round, and the process is uninterrupted.
>
> (Elizabeth Barrett Browning)

Many people, in many times and places, have enjoyed savouring and describing what it is like to create. The two nineteenth-century writers quoted here communicate intense aliveness and power. Mary Shelley was describing getting the idea for her novel *Frankenstein.* Victor Frankenstein, a medical student led astray by his fascination for 'unhallowed arts' discovers how to raise the dead, with dreadful consequences for himself and his family. The word 'unbidden' leaps out from her statement. She did not ask imagination to possess and guide her. She was merely open to that happening. A relationship is suggested between 'imagination' and 'mind' – from *mind* come the images, but from *imagination* comes their life.

And then look at the sudden intrusion of 'I' – the awe, the excitement, in the repeated 'I saw . . . I saw . . . I saw'. The passive awareness is suddenly the vividly active writer, poised to record the message. This is the moment of beginning. It is the moment when Mary Shelley's novel began. It is also the moment when the poem is there, demanding right of way.

Elizabeth Barrett Browning then describes what it feels like when 'the wheel goes round, and the process is uninterrupted': wholeness, fulfilment, aliveness.

First the poet gets the idea of the poem. Then comes the writing of it. Then there is a third stage. This is the communicating of it, the sharing of what has been written. The printed word – this book, for example – is about sharing what has been written.

Some writers profess not to care about what the world thinks; some actively seek fame; some wish to teach and influence the lives of others; some write to continue the work of those who have gone before; some write for those who come after them. But whatever their purposes in being writers, one thing is true for all of them: the poem must be shared, in whatever way is open to the writer.

Sharing the creative experience can be inspiring, and many writers have left a wealth of testimony for us to enjoy. It is clear that many nineteenth-century women writers found a personal fulfilment in writing that was not available to them in other areas of their lives as women and this is true for many women writing today. (This is not to suggest that women only used writing therapeutically. Very many wrote for professional success and critical esteem. Others wrote because they must. Different intentions overlap.) Because of this, women's writing may have a political dimension. How much is the *content* of what women produce created by the *context* of their lives, whether as nineteenth- or twentieth-century individuals? Many women who write do not wish to be identified as *women* writers. They will say that poetry is about that which is eternal: love, death, inspiration, nature, and so forth. It is not about gender and is no different from poetry written by men. Behind this belief may be another. Much criticism assumes that women's art — like women themselves — is second-rate. Space is now being given in some contemporary criticism to women's difficulties in starting to write. How much have women made society's implied criticism of their aspirations and purposes part of the fabric of their minds?

> Every time I sit down to write I get an almost overwhelming feeling of inadequacy. Who am I to be so presumptuous? What possible evidence do I have that this is something I can expect to do?
>
> (Anon., 1978)

> Unfortunately I seem to have a writer's block, I always do. Although I'd describe myself as reasonably confident in lots of situations I have no confidence when it comes to writing. There always seems to be a voice hovering around making sarcastic remarks. It's always a male voice. And it's always full of ridicule.
>
> (Anon., 1978)

Elizabeth Wolstenholme-Elmy, the Manchester campaigner for women's rights who became a suffragette in her seventies, wrote bitterly of 'the waste of woman worth that lived and died unknown'. (28) As one shares in the work of women who have been able to communicate their experience: poems, novels, newspaper articles, plays, letters, diaries, and so on, it is worth remembering the far greater numbers of women (and, of course, men) who have been, and who still are, denied full self-expression during their lives.

OF DICTIONARIES, INSPIRATION, AND THE MUSE

The *Oxford English Dictionary* gives three main figurative meanings for the word 'inspiration'. They show how words, and beliefs, can change. Initially, inspiration is 'influence of the spirit of God': the sense is purely religious. Later on, about the time of Shakespeare, we have: 'a breathing in or infusion of some idea, purpose, etc. into the mind; the suggestion, awakening of some feeling or impulse, especially of an exalted kind'. Later still, and certainly at the present time, the meaning is contained in phrases such as 'an inspired guess' or 'she was an inspiration to me'. The original religious, or almost religious, meaning is so diluted as to be almost non-existent.

So if we are to use this word to help us find out where poetry is coming from, perhaps we should go back to the way the images of Victor Frankenstein and his monstrous creation came into Mary Shelley's passive and receptive mind: 'My imagination, unbidden, possessed and guided me, gifting the successive images that arose in my mind with a vividness far beyond the usual bounds of reveries.'

Christians believe the Holy Spirit may enter the human soul and thus change or exalt the individual. Poets may believe that imagination, inspiration, or whatever, may come in as a distinct *other*. It may transform the whole geography of the poet's mind into something rich and strange. It may plant in her the overwhelming need to write, record, create. These two beliefs, or experiences, have much in common. But Christianity was not the first source of inspiration. Inspiration is one of humankind's most ancient experiences. What we call the Muse is the idea of inspiration expressed in the form of a woman. In pre-Christian times the idea of the Muse was still largely religious. She was one, three, four, or nine in number. She went by many names at different times and places. Some of these names reveal beliefs about the process of creation. Some ancient writers called the Muses Meditation, Remembrance, and Song. Others, Meditation, the Heart Delighting, Beginning and Song. Later writers called them the daughters of Memory, or the daughters of Time, said there were nine of them and assigned each one to a different art or branch of literature. The word 'Museum' originally meant 'place of the Muses'.

THE LITERATURE OF DESCRIPTION

Various writers, both literary critics and psychologists, have tried to describe the experience of inspiration. But describing an experience is not the same as having it. However, it can be helpful to know that an experience has been described. It is certainly interesting to be aware of the amount of agreement there is between writers who have attempted to describe the experience of inspiration. Essentially, the process the literature on inspiration describes is one of mental transformation. Obviously the experience will be interpreted differently by different people. What follows is real for me, and I have found my view supported by the testimony of many others.

Initially, the mental state is passive, unfocused, waiting. There is a feeling of vague yearning, restlessness, impatience. It is no different from the feeling of 'writer's block', except in one important particular: the writer believes that this state is the prelude to creation. The blocked writer doesn't.

Then, something comes: a formula, a phrase, an idea, a concept in the mind where only vagueness was before. The writer experiences a sudden release of energy, a sudden rush of enthusiasm.

From this *something* the poet can create an objective. Then comes the work of creating reality. It may not be a poem. The person experiencing the inspiration may be an artist, a musician, a doctor, a writer, a scientist, follow any kind of profession, or none.

Whatever the objective, after the experience of getting the idea, the work begins. Here the conscious processes need to start to work with the unconscious ones. There is a well-known saying, 'Genius is an infinite capacity for taking pains.' It is as true for inspiration. The writer needs not only to be able to experience the power of the imagination: she also needs in her craft a knowledge that is both wide and deep.

Poets themselves have attempted to communicate the experience in their poems. The reader will find examples in this book. One description is that of the early nineteenth-century poet and novelist Emily Brontë. In her poem, 'Julian M. and A.G. Rochelle' (9), she describes the mystical experiences of the woman prisoner, Rochelle. Though imprisoned in body she is free in mind, for an angel comes every night to her cell and offers her spirit liberty:

> But first a hush of peace, a soundless calm descends;
> The struggle of distress and fierce impatience ends;
> Mute music soothes my breast – unuttered harmony
> That I could never dream till earth was lost to me.
>
> Then dawns the Invisible, the Unseen its truth reveals
> My outward sense is gone, my inward essence feels
> Its wings are almost free, its home, its harbour found
> Measuring the gulf it stoops and dares the final bound!

SOME WAYS OF APPROACHING POETRY

I have tried to show that in every poem of quality there is, along with what it *says* it is about, the experience of what it was like for the author to create it. That experience is there for the reader to recreate and thus to share. Many people who love poetry love it because it speaks to them of their own experience. The poet may have words that describe their own experience better than they (believe they) could. To use an example from my own experience, the first poetry book I was ever given (a copy of the anthology I was then reading at school) is inscribed 'With delight that you have come to the realms of gold.' The phrase 'realms of gold' comes from a poem by John Keats in which he describes the intensely inspiring experience of reading Homer in a translation by the seventeenth-century poet, Chapman. Keats calls poetry 'the realms of gold'.

My mother, who gave me the poetry book, invariably recited A.E. Housman's poem about the cherry blossom in spring-time – the one that begins: 'Loveliest of trees, the cherry now, is hung with white along the bough'. In poetry, flowers have traditionally represented the brevity of youth and beauty. And so it is here. I have not much time left, says the poet. 'About the woodlands I will go,/And see the cherry hung with snow.' For me now, simple though it may be, that poem is part of the experience of spring blossom. When I see spring blossom, I remember that poem.

There are many poems in this book that may tell the truth about life experiences that may come to all of us at some time. Elizabeth Barrett Browning writing, as a middle-aged woman, of passionate romantic love in 'Bianca Among the Nightingales' (15) says:

> The cypress stood up like a church
>   That night we felt our love would hold,
> And saintly moonlight seemed to search
>   And wash the whole world clean gold;
> The olives crystallised the vales'
>   Broad slopes until the hills grew strong:
> The fire-flies and the nightingales
>   Throbbed each to either, flame and song,
> The nightingales, the nightingales!

Marina Tsvetayeva (presented here in Elaine Feinstein's translation) writes of the pain of abandonment in 'The Poem of the End' (77).

> Understand: we have
> grown into one as we slept and
> now I can't jump
> because I can't let go your hand
>
> and I won't be torn off
> as I press close to you: this
> bridge is no husband
> but a lover: a just slipping past
>
> our support: for the
> river is fed with bodies!
> I bite in like a tick
> you must tear out my roots to be rid of me

Using her native Australian landscape, Desirée Flynn writes of growing older (125):

> Soon I will climb the hill to the sunlight,
> from under the secret vines.
> Soon.
>
> But now seem rooted in the scented leaves,
> in the years of leaves, in the soft shadows
> where mountain ash and turpentine are talling to the sky.
>
> For this is how it is, the last parting,
> Now the last of my children is grown and gone,
> and the warm firelit circle is broken between the trees.
>
> Time ran a flash flood that rolled a creek to a river.
> Unbelieving, I stood on one side: they stood on the other.
>
> They waved, and ran fast to their gold-bright horizons;
> on their shimmering plain they grew small and far.
>
> It is dark here under the tree ferns.

Penelope Shuttle writes of the 'Expectant Mother' (74):

> I walk around the house
> in bare feet
> and a warm rope of blood
> links me to my child
>
> Rain falls on gardens and inscriptions
> but I hold the edge of the rain.
> I am a receptacle
> in which other rain, amniotic, gathers,
> for the one in his official residence
> to enjoy
>
> I think of the quiet use of the unborn eyelids
> and the stillness of my breasts that swell up,
> a warm procedure of strength.

When poetry communicates effectively, we get the idea that the experience is being recreated now. The poem's context is the moment in which we, the readers, experience the poem. Some poetry, though it may well seem vivid and immediate, brings with it a sense of the historical context in which it was created, the moment of 'now' it came from. Some of the poetry and songs in this book may evoke a vivid feeling of what it was like to be a woman in times gone by. For instance, during the late nineteenth and early twentieth centuries thousands of women in Britain campaigned with passionate commitment for the Vote. Though universal female suffrage was not granted until 1928, a partial victory was achieved in 1918. The suffragette anthem, 'The March of the Women' (33), composed by Cicely Hamilton and Ethel Smyth in 1911, records one of the most intensely militant phases of the suffrage campaign. We may be able to visualise hundreds or thousands of women singing this at a rally or march, in the early years of the twentieth century.

Long, long, we in the past,
Cowered in dread from the light of Heaven.
Strong, strong, stand we at last,
Fearless in faith and with sight new given.
Strength with its beauty, life with its duty,
(Hear the voice, oh, hear and obey),
These, these, beckon us on,
Open your eyes to the blaze of day!

Life, strife, these two are one!
Naught can ye win but by faith and daring.
On, on, that ye have done,
But for the work of today preparing.
Firm in reliance, laugh a defiance,
(Laugh in hope for sure is the end).
March, march, many as one,
Shoulder to shoulder and friend to friend.

Augusta Webster, an early campaigner for women's education and legal rights, used the figure of the 'fallen woman' as a mouthpiece for her own fierce anger at what it was like to be a woman, as she perceived it, in Britain in the 1860s. The long poem from which the extract in this book comes is called 'The Castaway' (22). The castaway, with no education to teach her any sense (her *brother* is the one who gets the education), drifts from governessing to prostitution. Marriage apart, there is nothing else for her, being a middle-class woman, and she is too poor to be marriageable. With savage irony, she denounces the lack of meaning and purpose in her life, and the lives of women like her. The poem created a sensation and made Augusta Webster famous.

Well, well, I know the wise ones talk and talk;
'Here's cause, here's cure:' 'No here it is and here:'
and find society to blame, or law,
the Church, the men, the women, too few schools,
too many schools, too much, too little taught:
somewhere or somehow someone is to blame:
but I say all the fault's with God himself
who puts too many women in the world.
We ought to die off reasonably and leave
as many as the men want, none to waste.
Here's cause; the woman's superfluity:
and for the cure, why, if it were the law,
say every year, in due percentages,
balancing them with men as the times need,

to kill off female infants, 'twould make room;
and some of us would not have lost too much,
losing life ere we know what it can mean.

So often we experience words as fast and empty things, rushing at and past us from television, newspapers, advertisements, packaging. We learn to ignore or rapidly digest this flood of verbiage. A new profession, that of information scientist, has been created. These people read books and articles for information and make their summaries available to those with no time to read the literature in full. To experience a poem, valuing and pondering each word, is to experience a different sort of communication. Everyday life may not support us in recognising the quality of the special kind of communication that poetry makes available to us. But those who seek will find.

ON THIS BOOK AS A WHOLE

Once, I wondered what part the editor played in the compilation of a poetry anthology. What had she done to get her name on the cover? Mistakenly, I supposed that compiling a poetry anthology simply meant selecting from what was there – reading a few books, picking out the ones editor (you) and publisher approved of; and there is something in this, though the few books quickly become an extraordinarily large number of books. But there is something more. Just like a literary critic, or indeed any kind of author, an anthologist writes a book. The fact that only a proportion of the total text was composed by her and her alone is, to a certain extent, immaterial.

Of course this extraordinary statement needs to be qualified right away. The purpose of an anthology should always be to celebrate the work of the writers collected within it, and this is certainly the purpose of *Bread and Roses*. The editor will, so far as it is within her powers, intend to represent honestly the literary output of the period her collection covers. A selection too full of personal idiosyncracies will lack credibility unless the editor is a very famous person whose personal quirks are in themselves of intrinsic interest. And it would be difficult – and pointless – to misrepresent text, authorship, date of composition, associated biographical data, etc., of any one specific poem.

But, still, an editor writes a book. While she strives honestly to represent and celebrate her chosen authors and to let them communicate unhindered the reality of what they have to say, she is nevertheless doing it in the context of a framework that she has created herself. It is not my intention now to go into this issue in a very profound way. Of course what I am presenting here implies a political position, a particular location in a context of time, class, race, even literary opinion. So does every book you've ever read, and this one is no exception. However, from a large number of possible approaches, I wish to select one.

No doubt, many poetry lovers will read this book from cover to cover. However, many who make use of anthologies (myself often included) do not do this. They prefer to dip into the book for individual favourites, for poems on a particular topic, from a particular historical moment, or by a particular author, or a particular section of the book. Fine. But what those who read a book like this may not be aware of is this: represented throughout *Bread and Roses* are a number of common themes, albeit expressed in very different ways.

As editor I am tempted to give you my opinion on every one of the poems in this book – naturally I have one – and so, were you to accept my opinion, every poem in this book would come to you via me. But more than fifty women writers are represented in this book and I feel strongly that I don't want to come between you and your experience of their work any more than I have already done by making this selection.

But I do believe that some of the general themes that came to me as I was compiling this book and that helped to make it what it is may provide some readers with strategies that enable them to experience the poetry more directly for themselves. So here is a selection.

First of all, what is the reader going to find in this book? *Bread and Roses* is divided into four sections. The first two sections, 'We Who Bleed' and 'A Vaster Knowledge', contain British poetry from the nineteenth and early twentieth centuries. The section 'We Who Bleed' concentrates on poetry largely literary in character; the section 'A Vaster Knowledge' contains much poetry coming from an awareness of great public happenings: the suffrage campaign, the struggle for women's education, the First World War. Of course the division is not rigid; at a time when women's right to education and professional training was a real political issue, women writers must have felt a strong urge to assert their right to use the language of the learned, whether classical quotation or progressive philosophy, and so much of the poetry of 'A Vaster Knowledge' is highly literary and full of learned allusion. Likewise, the poetry of 'We Who Bleed' isn't just personal emotion in a safe literary style: Elizabeth Barrett Browning, for example, was someone who set out to speak for her time and the reader will find issues like the anti-slavery struggle and the education of women recorded in this part of the book.

Another point about 'We Who Bleed': the student of English literature will know the names of Emily Brontë, Christina Rossetti, Elizabeth Barrett Browning, and their work is here. But what may be less well known is that the work of these valued and remembered writers is not 'typical Victorian poetry'. In the context of the time they were writing in, each one of them broke new ground.

It is to give a feeling of what was expected of a woman writer in early Victorian times that I have begun the collection with Felicia Hemans and Eliza Cook, writers well known and much admired in their day. Emily Brontë and her sisters knew and thought little of most of their popular contemporaries; I have not put Eliza Cook going on and on about her old straw hat (4) next to Emily Brontë writing of her other-worldly experiences of inspiration through her 'God of Visions' (5) by accident. The contrast is intended to startle, and even to shock. Contemporary readers certainly were shocked by the writings of the Brontë sisters. Perhaps this juxtaposition hints at why.

The second two sections in this book are called 'The Meeting' and 'The Renaming'. As before in 'We Who Bleed' the poets in 'The Meeting' are mainly those seeking to carry on a literary tradition. In some ways the poems of 'The Renaming' parallel those of 'A Vaster Knowledge'. The poems in this final section come from the present-day women's liberation movement and they raise some of the issues that confront those women who seek to make feminist politics an integral part of their lives. But, as before, areas of concern overlap. Women who are feminists confront the experiences of birth, death, motherhood, personal change, inspiration, friendship, and so forth, as do other women, and feminist writers share, like all writers, in the knowledge, whether conscious or unconscious, of a poetic tradition and the language that may be used to communicate it.

Of course this tradition isn't exclusively Western European, nor is it exclusively literary. In the limited space available in this book, the traditional songs telling of women's lives that Frankie Armstrong has collected and those she has composed let us know that there is a body of 'poetry' being handed down that's alive in performance and barely belongs on the printed page. The intensity of the Russian poet Marina Tsvetayeva, in Elaine Feinstein's translation, reminds us of those times and places where poetry has been and maybe still is very much a matter of life and death.

A minute fraction of the millions of women who have written, or wanted to write, or had something of their experience to record, are celebrated in this book. But why is this poetry there? What is the experience that made the space for the poem to come? Earlier, I have written of 'inspiration'. Later, there are suggestions for books to consult on the subject.

For me, I write because I like it. It's intensely enjoyable. For me, the experience of 'inspiration', of getting the words to communicate a new idea, is thrilling. As I have suggested before, I believe this experience to be one that all creative workers in whatever field at some time or another share. It is more often than not a private experience coming as it does when the writer is concentrating intensely on her task and, unless the writer has chosen to communicate it in unmistakable terms to her readers, they may not notice that it is there. The experience may remain the poet's secret.

Throughout the compilation of this book I have been very much aware of this 'secret' experience as a very real part of the excitement of poetry for me, so throughout the book the reader will find a fairly large number of poems that in one way or another intend to communicate some of the intensity of the experience from which poetry is created.

I begin the book with 'Corinne at the Capital' (1). Corinne, the heroine of a once intensely popular eighteenth-century novel (more of this later), is a genius at all the arts, but supreme in poetry which she is able to compose effortlessly on the spur of the moment. Here, the people of Rome celebrate her, a new kind of Roman Emperor, and in the excitement of the moment, inspiration comes:

All the spirit of thy sky
Now hath lit thy large dark eye,
And thy cheek a flush hath caught
From the *joy of kindled thought*
And the burning words of song
From thy lip flow fast and strong,
With a rushing stream's delight
In the freedom of its might. (my emphasis)

The expression may be antique, and too saccharine by half for modern tastes, but the experience being communicated is clear enough.

And Emily Brontë takes it further (9):

Then dawns the Invisible, the Unseen its truth reveals;
My outward sense is gone, my inward essence feels –
Its wings are almost free, its home, its harbour found;
Measuring the gulf it stoops and dares the final bound!

Amy Levy's Xantippe feels it die within her (24):

I fled across the threshold, hair unbound –
White garment stained to redness – beating heart
Flooded with all the flowing tide of hopes
Which once had gushed out golden, now sent back
Swift to their sources, never more to rise . . .

Mary Coleridge's witch is a frail but powerful spirit: the security of the home is no longer as it was to those who let her in (26):

Her voice was the voice that women have,
Who plead for their heart's desire
She came – she came – and the quivering flame
Sank and died in the fire.
It never was lit again on my hearth
Since I hurried across the floor,
To lift her over the threshold, and let her in
at the door!

Much modern poetry that is of value appears to share a common language of symbol and vision. This is the 'background of eternity' that Frances Cornford writes of in 'Summer Beach' (43). In this poetry are found seas, rivers and springs, gods, goddesses, angels and spirits, music, trees and moons, stars, dreams and monsters. (I am looking as I write through the third section of this book.) Many poets, writing independently, have approached the same themes. It is important to be clear that these themes are not chosen just to be pretty, or exotic, or 'poetical'. They are found as much in the poetry of centuries ago as in the poetry of today. Again and again, serious poets have taken these aspects of poetic tradition for their own use. These symbols are more than what they seem. Variously, they may represent mind, the unconscious, inspiration, the unknown, and more.

Stevie Smith's protagonist goes – like the Dante of the 'Inferno' – into the dark wood (48):

I rode with my darling in the dark wood at night
And suddenly there was an angel burning bright
Come with me or go far away he said
But do not stay alone in the dark wood at night.

My darling grew pale he was responsible
He said we should go back it was reasonable
But I wished to stay with the angel in the dark wood
at night.

Ruth Fainlight, like Emily Brontë, awaits the daemon (62):

Whatever I find if I search will be wrong.
I must wait: sternest trial of all, to contain myself,
Sit passive, receptive, and patient, empty
Of every demand and desire, until
That other, that being I never would have found
Though I spent my whole life in the quest, will step
Clear of the shadows, approach like a wild awkward child.

And still, for the committed feminist, the vision of what she may become carries on the idea of inspiration: 'oh let/the fierce goddess/

come', cries Michele Roberts's sibyl (88); and rebirth, recreation, begin in water. The ancient language of mythology carries the story forward.

Lucy, an unholy Alice
descends the precipice behind her shut eyelids
Lucy is not frightened: What frightens Lucy?
She is the Creatrix of the sea-bed light
the twisty weeds; the dear pulpy squids are hers
She knows what spangly and fearful construction
beckons from the bottom
(Diana Scott (94))

Water flooded everywhere
dripping over the edges of the plate of the world.
Spring stream rushing, impetuous white hurly-burly.
Slow-winding, green-pooled, golden-leaved in autumn.
Cart-track, thick mud carved by wheels,
black bowls laced with ice, glistening in the winter light.
(Catriona Stamp (92))

One day, without a warning tremor
the cloth danced.
Her fingers assuaged the silk thread with flame
and began something
that curled over the floor like the folds
of the Python.
...
Her hands were filament.
She finished eyes as large as saucers or millstones
(Judith Kazantzis (96))

These are brief examples of the sort of data that await the reader as she begins to explore what has been reported of inspiration; and the list may be extended almost indefinitely.

The writers represented in this book may have much in common in their deep literary concerns as do the greater multitude they must stand for. However, the century and a half this book covers is also a century and a half of substantial social change as far as the ordinary lives of women are concerned.

Literature isn't sociology; but the impressionistic picture literature gives of the times it comes from can be a valid one and can often be supported in due course by more factual evidence. So the frustrations and aspirations of, say, Aurora Leigh (14) or Xantippe (24), of the struggles of the women's rights campaigners against resistance and prejudice (33, and others) can lead us directly to an awareness of the times these characters inhabited. They create a context for getting the idea of what it may have been like to experience life as a nineteenth-century woman. Even the slender biographical notes and references that support the various texts here are evidence in themselves of a shift in the possibilities of self-expression in the lives of women, when you contrast some aspects of the lives of present-day women writers with their nineteenth-century counterparts.

Present days, past times; creating literature, creating polemic, finding self-expression – all of it poetry, and all of it valuable as poetry. Some will disagree. Some very distinguished contemporary voices have asserted that poetry is *not* the autobiography of the artist, nor the history of the artist's times. Poetry's proper concern is for matters eternal – love, death, the mind, the spirit, the meaning of dreams, the aspirations of the human soul, and so on; matters that do not change from generation to generation. For myself, I choose at the present time not to make judgements about what poetry is and to be aware rather of the quality of the ways I experience poetry coming from different times and concerns.

I am aware, for example, of a distinct shift in content and expression between the poetry that expresses some of the concerns of the nineteenth- and early twentieth-century campaigners for women's rights, and the poetry coming from the present-day women's liberation movement. The juxtaposition can be revealing, for the situations that created these poems have a number of aspects in common.

From 1867:

> Well, well, the silly rules this silly world
> makes about women! This is one of them.
> Why must there be pretence of teaching them
> what no one ever cares that they should know
> what, grown out of the schoolroom, they cast off
> like the schoolroom pinafore, no better fit
> for any use of real grown up life,
> for any use of her who seeks and waits
> the husband and the home, for any use,
> for any shallowest pretence of use,
> to her who has them?

(Augusta Webster (22))

From 1980:

> I've seen too much dissension,
> too much strife, too much despair,
> and still I wait to celebrate
> the sisterhood we share.
>
> To know again that all my pain
> is not confined to me;
> that other women share the hurt,
> that though our lives take root in dirt
> we still grow strong and free.

> This one more thing I'll tell you sister,
> then I have to go;
> if anger is our weapon, then
> be careful where you throw.
>
> If anger is our weapon
> don't ignite it showing off.
> for anger is explosive, and
> right now it's going off.
> (Stephanie Markman (136))

The poems of 'A Vaster Knowledge' read to me for the most part like messages from the front line. A terrible anger, almost too painful to be borne, burns in the pages of poems like 'The Castaway' (22) and 'Xantippe' (24). It is rage that sustains these women in the struggle; fear surrounds them, but a grandiose vision, untested as yet against any everyday reality, leads them on: 'Till clothed with majesty of mind she stand/Regent of Nature's will, in heart, in head, in hand' (28).

Feminist women today may still need to defend their rights, though a limited amount of serious reporting of feminist issues is now observable here and there in the public media, which may bring changes. But what is transmitted often in present-day feminist poetry is, rather than the intention to create a space for women, the need to explore a space which has already been created. The 'Ancient Feminist' has, for all her pain, new words in her vocabulary: 'sister', 'sisterhood' – and she is able to take them for granted. The feminist idea that all women are sisters would have been unknown to the lonely castaway. And when the 'Ancient Feminist' speaks of celebrating the sisterhood we share she is talking about something slightly different from the 'shoulder to shoulder/and friend to friend' of the 'March of the Women' (33). Celebrating sisterhood doesn't just mean going into battle together; it means also the possibility of exploring quite everyday issues from a feminist point of view – for 'the personal is political'. And, as I'll suggest later, in the context of the historical prejudices that have in the past restricted literary women very largely to accepted womanly forms of literary self-expression, for a woman today to write of her love for her mother, or for other women, or of her body, or of her righteous anger, is, even if on a small scale, a political gesture.

The 'literary' poetry of the Victorian age comes, for the most part, from a context of belief about poetry that no longer exists in Britain. Throughout the greater part of the Victorian era – though the novel was certainly taking over – academic and literary opinion still believed poetry to be the most noble of the literary arts, the one most fitted to articulate the age's deepest concerns. Though this ancient belief, which goes back many centuries, was in the nineteenth century fast dying out, Alfred Lord Tennyson could still be called Bard. The nineteenth century was to see the novel supersede poetry as the medium for serious literature, a position that the novel perhaps holds even today (though some would argue, and plausibly, that the novel's pre-eminence has in its turn been overtaken by the immediacy of film). This is the context in which the nineteenth-century women poets were writing – but there was something more: poetry was a very serious literary art, certainly, but serious only for men. Women writing in those days wrote in the context of a mass of expectations and judgements and prejudices about what writing as a woman meant. Elizabeth Barrett Browning mocks expectations about women's writing in the extract from *Aurora Leigh*, reproduced below (14):

> Not as mere work but as mere woman's work
> Expressing the comparative respect
> Which means the absolute scorn. 'Oh, excellent,
> What grace, what facile turns, what fluent sweeps,
> What delicate discernment . . . almost thought!
> The book does honour to the sex, we hold.
> Among our female authors we make room
> For this fair writer, and congratulate
> The country that produces in these times
> Such women, competent to . . . spell.'

The tone of Victorian literary criticism, as applied to many a woman's writing is, incidentally, precisely reproduced here.

So, a double bind: writing poetry was a serious and noble art but writing as a woman was by definition inane and superficial. Defining something in the opposition's terms has never been a fruitful exercise. However, an awareness of the context in which women's poetry of the Victorian era was being created can support us in understanding the heroism of Emily Brontë or Emily Dickinson in disdaining popular opinion and writing for themselves; or the immense effort and years of home study that enabled Elizabeth Barrett Browning to write on the 'male' scale; or the expertise with which Felicia Hemans exploited popular taste to financial reward; or the skill with which Christina Rossetti, while writing poetry of great contemporary appeal, never compromised her personal integrity or disguised her personal voice.

It would be true to say that most serious present-day poets are working in a situation where public recognition of poetry as a serious art form no longer exists. A fairly contemporary generation of present-day writers are represented in the poems of 'The Meeting'. In their work, to a varying degree, and more explicitly in the work of the earlier generation of writers (active in the thirties and forties and perhaps still writing now), is an intention to recreate and hand on to their successors some of the traditional symbolic language and standards of excellence that they believe to be an integral part of the true nature of poetry.

They are concerned with the experience of vision, and with the process of recreating it in words. The poet of today may be a lonely hero; lacking any substantial acknowledgment of a public role – other than whatever modest public life she can create for herself – her own dedication to her art and to the excellence she sees in it keeps her, often unrewarded, on her ancient, lonely road. The vision remains, as Elaine Feinstein tells us (60):

and now in streets where only white
mac or car metal catches the falling
light, if we sing of
the red and the blue and the texture of goat hair
there is no deceit in our prophecy:
for even now our brackish waters can
be sweetened by a strange tree.

And Jenny Joseph knows that the entry into mystery and marvel is only just outside our familiar world (66):

Mole he sleeps deep, his velvet nurtured by
The proper dryness, cohesion, in the earth
His only place, he knows,
Safe from the pull of the malign dews of the stars
The vast cold glitter, thin twanging in the spheres
That draws men, crazy, across shadeless tundra.

Present and past times assist in recreating each other. Juxtaposing common experiences from past and present creates a dialogue, a drama. Poetry and drama, after all, have the same roots. I like high drama; I like literature that excites and moves me. I have consciously chosen many of the poems in this book – though I hasten to add that humour, documentary, meditation, and so on, have certainly not been excluded – to create a feeling of intensity, of drama. These poems are there to be reacted to. Poetry, as I believe, may certainly be *about* inspiration – an experience of intense emotion and, as Corinne has it, 'kindled thought' – but poetry has always *been* an inspiration to many people in different times and places. This is as it should be; for when this happens the experience of the inspiration that created the poem is, however briefly, shared by those who read it. And the reading of the poem, however fleeting it may be in terms of time, contributes profoundly, I believe, to the quality of their lives.

FURTHER READING

Brewster Ghiselin (ed.), *The Creative Process: A Symposium*, University of California Press, 1946.
Rosamund Harding, *An Anatomy of Inspiration*, Hefter, 1940.
Maurice Bowra, *Inspiration and Poetry*, Macmillan & Co., London, 1955.
Robert Graves, *The White Goddess*, Faber & Faber, 3rd edn, 1952.
Kathleen Raine, *Defending Ancient Springs*, Oxford University Press, 1967.
Penelope Shuttle and Peter Redgrove, *The Wise Wound: Menstruation and Everywoman*, Victor Gollancz, 1978.

We Who Bleed

WOMEN'S POETRY 1820–60

Radiant daughter of the sun!
Now thy living wreath is won
Crown'd of Rome! – Oh! art thou not
Happy in that glorious lot?
Felicia Hemans (1)

Thought followed thought – star followed star
Through boundless regions on
While one sweet influence, near and far
Thrilled through and proved us one.
Emily Brontë (6)

Our wounds are different. Your white men
Are after all, not gods indeed
Nor able to make Christ's again
Do good with bleeding. *We* who bleed
(Stand off) we help not in our loss!
We are too heavy for our cross
And fall and crush you and your seed.
Elizabeth Barrett Browning (12)

Women as you are
Mere women, personal and passionate
You give us doating mothers and perfect wives,
Sublime Madonnas, and enduring saints!
We get no Christ from you – and verily
We shall not get a poet, in my mind.
Elizabeth Barrett Browning (14)

They seem very far away. They are neither our mothers, nor our grandmothers: they are, perhaps, our great-great-grandmothers. Measured against the span of human history, four or five generations may not seem so long. But in terms of increased possibilities and raised expectations for women, it is enormous. Nevertheless, beneath the archaic language and obscure references, perfectly recognisable dilemmas are being articulated. Take, for example, fame.

The first poem in this collection is called 'Corinne at the Capitol'. Corinne is the heroine of a famous eighteenth-century novel, *Corinne*, by Madame de Staël who appears to have entered into the fantasy life of every nineteenth-century literary woman. And why? Corinne is gifted in all the arts, but in poetry and music she is a supreme genius. She can do everything. Moreover, she is universally honoured and acknowledged by *everybody* for it. And publicly, too. This fantasy is powerful enough *now*; think what it must have meant to a nineteenth-century woman who had often to conceal the fact that she wrote, published more often than not under a male pseudonym or anonymously, and had often to put much energy into reconciling being 'womanly' with her 'unwomanly' drive for distinction.

The most famous scene in the book, and the one that most caught the imagination of its readers, is that of Corinne's triumph in Rome. Like an ancient Roman emperor, Corinne is drawn in triumph through the streets. The Roman people acclaim her and shower her with flowers. She ascends the steps of the Capitol. At her moment of supreme triumph, words spring to her lips, and raising her lyre, she begins to compose spontaneously (1).

Thou hast gained the summit now
Music hails thee from below; –

Now afar it rolls – it dies –
And thy voice is heard to rise
With a low and lovely tone
In its thrilling power alone;
And thy lyre's deep silvery string
Touch'd as by a breeze's wing
Murmurs tremblingly at first
Ere the tide of rapture burst.

And thy cheek a flush hath caught
From the joy of kindled thought;
And the burning words of song
From thy lip flow fast and strong,
With a rushing stream's delight
In the freedom of its might.

The poet is describing the moment of inspiration, doubtless as she herself experienced it – but she sets it firmly in a dramatic situation. Instant visibility and instant acclaim: the process of creation, of full self-expression is not private, hidden, denied – it is public, effortless, pleasurable and, even better, rewarded. But what the poet is describing is almost entirely fantasy. Though a modest amount of public life – talks, readings, lectures, reviewing; and there is evidence of this later in this collection – may reward the modern literary woman, her nineteenth-century counterpart would have received little or none. Weren't women private beings? Felicia Hemans finished her poem of the triumph of Corinne in the following way:

Happier, happier far than thou,
With the laurel on thy brow,
She that makes the humblest hearth
Lovely but to one on earth!

Captain Hemans had left his gifted wife to be the sole support of a family of five after six years of marriage, and Mrs Hemans (as she preferred to be called) did receive a fair amount of public acclaim in her day. It seems hard to believe that she could have entered so wholeheartedly into Corinne's joy and then sincerely asserted that being a stay-at-home wife and mother was a far greater joy. Yet that was the received wisdom of the time; and the continual tension between the striving spirit of the artist, as strong and assertive as the artist must be, and the public 'image' of the Victorian middle-class woman happy to be at home doing nothing in particular was one that a nineteenth-century woman had constantly to cope with.

Women writers of this period – and we are talking now about work written in the middle years of the nineteenth century – were poignantly aware of their isolation. On the other hand, they read, they studied, they educated themselves, they were often aware of each other's works. Very, very occasionally a writer might venture out on to the public stage, might even meet her publishers; and of course they gained heart and encouragement and inspiration and felt themselves in touch with the mind of their time – but even so . . . They have quite a lot to tell us about being alone.

> I dwell alone – I dwell alone, alone
> Whilst full my river flows down to the sea,
> Gilded with flashing boats
> That bring no friend to me:
> O love-songs gurgling from a thousand throats,
> O love-pangs, let me be.

cried Christina Rossetti (20); and someone who sees in this just a miserable woman wanting to be loved is missing a lot. There is the craft of the poem – the sounds, the rhythms, the meticulous choice of words; there's the powerful central image. The river, flowing down to the sea, has traditionally been a symbol of life moving towards eternity: but water, too, from which we all came, has always been the element of the unconscious, of the imagination, in the language of poetry and dream. What are these gilded, ornate boats moving on the mighty river? Could they be her poetry? But the 'flashing boats' bring her no friend.

There's obviously more here than personal alienation; there's a struggle to come to terms with a world that does not acknowledge you; you launch ships on the deep, cast your bread upon the waters and nothing – so far as you can see – ever returns.

In an early scene of her verse epic *Aurora Leigh* about the successful career of a woman poet, Elizabeth Barrett Browning included a direct reference to the famous triumph of Corinne. Alone in the garden, on the morning of her birthday, Aurora, 'woman and poet', crowns *herself*, and *no one* is there. No cheering throngs, no triumph for Aurora, yet. But someone is there – cousin Romney, who has been observing her in secret, and what he has to say about women's poetry and women's politics you can read (14). Aurora is certainly a match for him; but it is surely significant that the woman crowns herself, alone, and far from the cheering hordes of Rome, and that the only observer is a man, all set to destroy her with words:

> There it is! –
> You play beside a death bed like a child,
> Yet measure to yourself a prophet's place
> To teach the living. None of all these things
> Can women understand. You generalise
> Oh, nothing, – not even grief!

Finally, this Utopian socialist declares:

> Therefore, this same world
> Uncomprehended by you, must remain
> Uninfluenced by you.

Aurora, by crowning herself, is saying 'even if nobody takes pride in me, I will take pride in myself, for I am valuable', and Emily Brontë's famous poem 'No Coward Soul Is Mine' (7) disdains the world's opinion in a gesture that goes much further:

> Vain are the thousand creeds
> That move men's hearts, unutterably vain,
> Worthless as withered weeds
> Or idlest froth amid the boundless main
>
> To waken doubt in one
> Holding so fast by thy infinity . . .

On one level, the expression is traditionally religious, but for Emily Brontë, who wrote throughout her life of the Spirit who inspired her in both literary and religious terms, it surely meant much more than that; and its power, its arrogance, its sheer self-belief carry a compelling message.

The human spirit had a lot to triumph over if you were a nineteenth-century woman. Education for women was on the whole designed to keep them ignorant. Elizabeth Barrett Browning took on this theme in *Aurora Leigh* (14). Aurora describes her education as having as its purpose to develop in women a 'potential faculty in everything/ of abdicating power in it', that is, failing gracefully. And there is more:

> By the way,
> The works of women are symbolical.
> We sew, sew, prick our fingers, dull our sight
> Producing what? A pair of slippers, sir,
> To put on when you're weary – or a stool
> To stumble over and vex you . . . 'curse that stool!'
> . . . Alas, alas!
> This hurts most, this – that, after all, we are paid
> The worth of our work, perhaps.

Women knew their chains. Many nineteenth-century feminists followed the anti-slavery struggle then going on in the United States and felt keenly the parallels they perceived between the chattel status of the black slaves and their own dependency and powerlessness.

Elizabeth Barrett Browning's anti-slavery poem, 'The Runaway Slave at Pilgrim's Point' (12), published in an American anti-slavery paper to help the abolitionist cause, draws together the themes of oppression by class, sex and race in the figure of the black woman whose lover is sold down river. She is raped by her white master and bears a child 'far too white, too white for me'. She escapes, murders the baby, buries him in the forest and takes refuge on Pilgrim's Point, where the first white settlers landed in search of 'freedom'. The final tableau sees her confronting the man sent out to recapture her and mete out punishment. She cries:

> Our wounds are different. Your white men
> Are after all, not gods indeed,
> Nor able to make Christ's again
> Do good with bleeding. *We* who bleed
> (Stand off!) we help not in our loss!
> *We* are too heavy for our cross,
> And fall and crush you and your seed.

A tragic poem, but there is a searing anger in it too. Elizabeth Barrett Browning, from her privileged position as an educated woman of the upper classes, with unlimited time to study, write and develop as a writer, pays an honourable debt to all less fortunate women. It is an acknowledgement of privilege and of responsibility which has a counterpart in Christina Rossetti's 'A Royal Princess' (21), another campaigning poem, which was written as a contribution to a fund-raising book to relieve distress among Lancashire millworkers. In it, the princess gradually becomes aware that her family's wealth is based on exploitation of the working people and discovers that she is supposed to be little more than decoration in the palace. She resolves to throw in her lot with the people.

But there are some imprisonments that cannot, even in fantasy, end; and much poetry of this period is concerned with strategies of spiritual freedom: the creation of an inner space, so real, so potent in its magic that the conditions in which the poets lived and worked are transcended. This is not to say that such poetry rushes to take refuge in Cloud-cuckoo-land: far from it. At its best it brings the struggle, the process of the transcendence and the transcendence itself clearly before our eyes (7).

> No coward soul is mine
> No trembler in the world's storm-troubled sphere
> I see Heaven's glories shine
> And Faith shines equal arming me from Fear . . .

Though Earth and Moon were gone
And suns and universes ceased to be
And thou wert left alone
Every Existence would exist in thee

There is not room for Death
Nor atom that his might could render void
Since thou art Being and Breath
And what thou art may never be destroyed.

The Poets

FELICIA HEMANS | 1783–1835 (1) (2). Felicia Hemans was born in Liverpool, the daughter of a merchant. When Felicia was seven years old, her father's business difficulties forced a move to more rural and romantic Wales, which she later regarded as a turning-point in her life. She was educated at home by her mother who considered her a prodigy. However, when her youthful verses were published in 1808, public opinion was not kind. But, it brought her fame of a sort and the poet Shelley tried to strike up a correspondence, to which Felicia's mother hastened to put a stop. In 1812 Felicia married Captain Albert Hemans and the couple lived first in Northamptonshire, then with her parents. They had five children in little more than six years and then, for an unrevealed reason, Captain Hemans departed for Italy and the couple never met again, though they are said to have corresponded about their children. It was a fortunate time to be a poet – there was great popular demand for poetry and Felicia's poetry perfectly embodied the romantic sensibility of the time in thoroughly respectable form. She found herself able to support and educate her children through her writing and took a pride in so doing. Many volumes of her poetry were published; she won prizes in poetry writing and wrote magazine essays and plays. In 1825 a separate American edition of her work was issued and she was even offered the editorship of a Boston magazine, which she did not accept. In 1827 her mother, to whom she was devoted, died. Felicia Hemans apparently offered to rejoin her husband, but he would not have it. She took pleasure in travel and enjoyed some of the rewards of fame; she met the literary giants of the day, including Scott and Wordsworth for whom she had the greatest admiration. However her health was failing; she moved to London to live with one of her brothers and, in 1835, a venerated but sorrowing woman, she died.

ELIZA COOK 1818–89 (3) (4). Eliza Cook was born in London, the youngest of eleven children of a brazier. In 1827 her father retired from business and the family moved to a farm in Sussex. Eliza Cook is said to have been entirely self-educated. As a young woman she submitted poems anonymously to papers, especially one called the *Weekly Despatcher* whose proprietor became curious about her identity. He advertised for the unknown contributor to reveal her identity and, when she did so, he made her a regular contributor. From 1849–54 she edited 'Eliza Cook's Journal', but the newspaper unfortunately collapsed. Her own personal popularity was constant and unfailing, especially with those readers who would have found nothing for them in the serious literature of the day. Her best-known poem, 'The Old Arm-chair', was written in memory of her mother and is reproduced in this collection. The work of Felicia Hemans and Eliza Cook contrasts strongly with those whom we remember as the 'greats' of the nineteenth-century – Emily Brontë, Elizabeth Barrett Browning, Christina Rossetti, but it is important to remember that the work of the former conformed far more closely to conventional expectations of women's writing, whereas the 'great' writers were all in their differing ways quite atypical.

EMILY BRONTE 1818–48 (5) (6) (7) (8) (9) (10) (11). Emily Brontë was two years younger than Charlotte, and a year and a half older than Anne. Emily was born in Thornton, Yorkshire, and moved in early childhood to Haworth, where her father became curate. With Charlotte and her two oldest sisters, Emily was sent in 1824 to the Clergy Daughters' School at Cowan Bridge. Maria and Elizabeth died in an epidemic that broke out in the school and Charlotte and Emily were rescued just in time. Throughout her life Emily associated restraint with torture. In 1835 she found three months at Roe Head School near Halifax a great strain; in 1837, she acted as governess to a family in Halifax, but six months was all she could bear. In 1842, the three surviving sisters had the idea of opening a small school in their own home and, in order to improve their qualifications, Emily accompanied Charlotte to the Pensionaat Héger in Brussels where she stayed nine months. Apart from a trip to York with Anne, the rest of her life was passed in Haworth, then an isolated moorland village. In 1845, Charlotte discovered the manuscripts of Emily's poems which she had hitherto kept secret. Together, the three sisters decided on publication under pseudonyms and the *Poems of Currer, Ellis and Acton Bell* appeared in 1846. Emily's marvellous novel, *Wuthering Heights*, was published in an edition with Anne's *Agnes Grey* in 1847. Emily died three months after her beloved brother Branwell at the age of thirty. Her modern biographer, Winifred Guerin, offers the moving and plausible hypothesis that Emily's daemon, the spirit that she writes of repeatedly in her poetry which had inspired her poetry and given meaning both to her outward and inner life, appeared to have deserted her and that her will to live went with him. Emily's poems fall into two main kinds – narratives of her fantasy land of Gondal and narratives of her own spiritual and mystical journeys.

ELIZABETH BARRETT BROWNING 1806–61 (12) (13) (14) (15). Elizabeth Barrett was born in Durham, the eldest of eleven children; but when she was very young the family moved to 'Hope End', a large house in Herefordshire and this is where she spent her childhood and girlhood. She was truly precocious and apparently learned to read Greek with assurance at the age of eight. Her juvenile epic, the

Battle of Marathon, was privately printed by her father when she was twelve. She suffered a severe fall from a horse when she was fifteen. When she was twenty her mother died, her father experienced financial difficulties and the family moved first to Sidmouth, then to that famous address, 50 Wimpole Street in London, and her cloistered years began. Modern biographers diagnose specific medical causes to explain the years of invalidism that followed but, given the change in the family circumstances, her father's jealous and tyrannical behaviour, her brother's tragic drowning at Torquay, psychological factors must have contributed. Despite this, she spent the ensuing years in energetic and committed study and in writing and her writing gradually made her a national figure. In 1846 the family friend John Kenyon brought Robert Browning to call. He had been fascinated by her work and her reputation – until her death to be consistently greater than his – and romantic feeling quickly grew. Elizabeth's father became jealous and suspicious and, when Elizabeth perceived his intention to separate them, she acted decisively. She secretly married Robert Browning on 12 September 1846 and a week later they left for France and then Italy where they were to live for fifteen years, until she died. Her father never forgave her, refused to see her again, never even acknowledged her overtures – as far as he was concerned his daughter was dead. The invalid was marvellously rejuvenated, once away from her family. Half a dozen more volumes of poetry were produced, including *Aurora Leigh* in 1857 which was immensely successful, and her marriage was loving and supportive. Her son was born in 1849. She had taken an informed interest in politics all her life and during her life in Italy took a committed interest in the struggles then going on to liberate Italy from Austrian rule. She died very suddenly in 1861 and is buried in the English Cemetery in Florence.

CHRISTINA ROSSETTI 1830–94 (16) (17) (18) (19) (20) (21). Christina Rossetti was the youngest of the Rossetti brothers and sisters. She was born in London's Charlotte Street (now Hallam Street). Her father was a political refugee from Naples; her mother was also of Italian extraction. Christina Rossetti was educated at home and her first volumes of poetry were privately printed when she was twelve and seventeen. When the Pre-Raphaelite group started in 1849, four of Christina's poems were printed in their magazine, *The Germ*. In the 1850s her father's health failed and the family faced actual poverty. Dante Gabriel worked as an artist; but William Michael Rossetti had a steady job in the civil service, which brought in some money. Maria worked as a governess and Christina gave Italian lessons. Apart from occasional visits to the country and one to Italy, Christina's life was spent entirely in the city – and at home with her mother and sister. Religious differences – she was very devout – came between her and marriage on two occasions. Her later poetry and prose is devotional in character. Today she is best remembered for poems from her two early volumes, *Goblin Market and Other Poems* (1862) and *The Prince's Progress and Other Poems* (1866). In 1873 she contracted Grave's disease and died of cancer at the age of sixty-four.

Felicia Hemans

CORINNE AT THE CAPITOL (1)

'The ladies should be thinking that there is, in the career of Corinne, nothing that could equal the secluded life of a beloved spouse, of a joyous mother' – (*Madame de Staël*)*

Daughter of th'Italian heaven!
Thou, to whom its fires are given,
Joyously thy car hath rolled
Where the conquerors pass'd of old;
And the festal sun that shone,
O'er three hundred triumphs gone
Makes thy day of glory bright,
With a shower of golden light.

Now thou tread'st th'ascending road,
Freedom's foot so proudly trod;
While, from tombs of heroes borne
From the dust of empire shorn,
Flowers upon thy graceful head,
Chaplets of all hues, are shed,
In a soft and rosy rain,
Touched with many a gemlike stain.

Thou hast gained the summit now!
Music hails thee from below; –
Music, whose rich notes might stir
Ashes of the sepulchre;
Shaking with victorious notes
All the bright air as it floats.
Well may woman's heart beat high
Unto that proud harmony!

Now afar it rolls – it dies –
And thy voice is heard to rise
With a low and lovely tone
In its thrilling power alone;

(*F.H. gives this quotation in the original French. It is translated for the modern reader's convenience.)

And thy lyre's deep silvery string,
Touch'd as by a breeze's wing,
Murmurs tremblingly at first,
Ere the tide of rapture burst.

All the spirit of thy sky
Now hath lit thy large dark eye,
And thy cheek a flush hath caught
From the joy of kindled thought;
And the burning words of song
From thy lip flow fast and strong,
With a rushing stream's delight
In the freedom of its might.

Radiant daughter of the sun!
Now thy living wreath is won.
Crown'd of Rome! – Oh! art thou not
Happy in that glorious lot? –
Happier, happier far than thou,
With the laurel on thy brow,
She that makes the humblest hearth
Lovely but to one on earth!

(2) TO THE POET WORDSWORTH

Thine is a strain to read amongst the hills,
The old and full of voices – by the source
Of some free stream, whose gladdening presence fills
The solitude with sound – for in its course
Even such is thy deep song, that seems a part
Of those high scenes, a fountain from their heart.

Or its calm spirit fitly may be taken
To the still breast, in some sweet garden-bowers,
Where summer winds each tree's low tones awaken,
And bud and bell with changes mark the hours.
There let thy thoughts be with me, while the day
Sinks with a golden and serene decay.

Or by some hearth where happy faces meet,
When night hath hush'd the woods with all their birds,
There, from some gentle voice, that lay were sweet
As antique music, linked with household words.
While, in pleased murmurs, woman's lip might move,
And the raisèd eye of childhood shine in love.

Or where the shadows of dark solemn yews
Brood silently o'er some lone burial ground,
Thy verse hath power that brightly might diffuse
A breath, a kindling, as of Spring, around,
From its own glow of hope and courage high,
And steadfast faith's victorious constancy.

True bard and holy! – Thou art e'en as one
Who, by some secret gift of soul or eye,
In every spot beneath the smiling sun,
Sees where the springs of living waters lie –
Unseen awhile they sleep – till, touched by thee,
Bright healthful waves flow forth, to each glad wanderer
free!

Eliza Cook

(3) THE OLD ARM-CHAIR

I love it, I love it; and who shall dare
To chide me for loving that old arm-chair?
I've treasured it long as a sainted prize;
I've bedew'd it with tears, and embalm'd it with sighs.
'Tis bound by a thousand bands to my heart;
Not a tie will break, not a link will start.
Would ye learn the spell? – a mother sat there;
And a sacred thing is that old arm-chair.

In Childhood's hour I linger'd near
The hallow'd seat with listening ear;
And gentle words that mother would give;
To fit me to die, and teach me to live.
She told me shame would never betide,
With truth for my creed and God for my guide;
She taught me to lisp my earliest prayer;
As I knelt beside that old arm-chair.

I sat and watch'd her many a day,
When her eye grew dim, and her locks were grey;
And I almost worshipp'd her when she smiled,
And turn'd from her Bible, to bless her child.
Years roll'd on; but the last one sped –
My idol was shatter'd; my earth-star fled:
I learnt how much the heart can bear,
When I saw her die in that old arm-chair.

'Tis past, 'tis past, but I gaze on it now
With quivering breath and throbbing brow:
'Twas there she nursed me; 'twas there she died:
And Memory flows with lava tide.
Say it is folly, and deem me weak,
While the scalding drops start down my cheek;
But I love it, I love it; and cannot tear
My soul from a mother's old arm-chair.

MY OLD STRAW HAT (4)

1

Farewell, old friend, – we part at last;
Fruits, flowers, and summer, all are past,
And when the beech-leaves bid adieu,
My Old Straw Hat must vanish too.
We've been together many an hour,
In grassy dell and garden bower;
And plait and riband, scorch'd and torn,
Proclaim how well thou hast been worn,
We've had a time, gay, bright, and long;
So let me sing a grateful song, –
And if one bay-leaf falls to me,
I'll stick it firm and fast in thee,
My Old Straw Hat.

2

Thy flapping shade and flying strings
Are worth a thousand close-tied things.
I love thy easy-fitting crown;
Thrust lightly back, or slouching down.
I cannot brook a muffled ear,
When lark and blackbird whistle near;
And dearly like to meet and seek
The fresh wind with unguarded cheek.
Toss'd in a tree, thou'lt bear no harm;
Flung on the moss, thou'lt lose no charm;
Like many a real friend on earth,
Rough usage only proves thy worth.
My Old Straw Hat.

3

The world will stare at those who wear
Rich snowy pearls in raven hair;
And diamonds flash bravely out
In chesnut tresses wreathed about;
The golden bands may twine and twirl,

Like shining snakes, through each fair curl;
And soft down with imperial grace
May bend o'er Beauty's blushing face:
But much I doubt if brows that bear
The jewell'd clasp and plumage rare,
Or temples bound with crescent wreath,
Are half so cool as mine beneath
My Old Straw Hat.

4

Minerva's helmet! what of that?
Thou'rt quite as good, my Old Straw Hat;
For I can think, and muse, and dream,
With poring brain and busy scheme;
I can inform my craving soul
How wild bees work and planets roll;
And be all silent, grave, and grim,
Beneath the shelter of thy brim.
The cap of Liberty, forsooth!
Thou art the thing to me in truth;
For slavish fashion ne'er can break
Into the green paths where I take
My Old Straw Hat.

5

My Old Straw Hat, my conscience tells
Thou has been hung with Folly's bells;
Yet Folly rings a pleasant chime,
If the rogue will but 'mind his time',
And not come jingling on the way
When sober minstrels ought to play.
For oft when hearts and eyes are light,
Old Wisdom should keep out of sight.
But now the rustic bench is left,
The tree of every leaf bereft,
And merry voices, all are still,
That welcomed to the well-known hill
My Old Straw Hat.

6

Farewell, old friend, thy work is done;
The misty clouds shut out the sun;
The grapes are pluck'd, the hops are off,
The woods are stark, and I must doff
My Old Straw Hat – but 'bide a wee',
Fair skies we've seen, yet we may see
Skies full as fair as those of yore,
And then we'll wander forth once more.
Farewell, till drooping bluebells blow,
And violets stud the warm hedgerow –
Farewell, till daisies deck the plain –
Farewell, till spring days come again –
My Old Straw Hat!

(5) O THY BRIGHT EYES MUST ANSWER NOW

O thy bright eyes must answer now,
When Reason, with a scornful brow,
Is mocking at my overthrow;
O thy sweet tongue must plead for me
And tell why I have chosen thee!

Stern Reason is to judgement come
Arrayed in all her forms of gloom;
Wilt thou my advocate be dumb?
No, radiant angel, speak and say
Why I did cast the world away;

Why have I persevered to shun
The common paths that others run;
And on a strange road journeyed on
Heedless alike of Wealth and Power –
Of Glory's wreath and Pleasure's flower.

These once indeed seemed Beings divine,
And they perchance heard vows of mine
And saw my offerings on their shrine –
But, careless gifts are seldom prized,
And mine were worthily despised;

So with a ready heart I swore
To seek their altar-stone no more,
And gave my spirit to adore
Thee, ever present, phantom thing –
My slave, my comrade, and my King!

A slave because I rule thee still;
Incline thee to my changeful will
And make thy influence good or ill –
A comrade, for by day and night
Thou art my intimate delight –

My Darling Pain that wounds and sears
And wrings a blessing out from tears

By deadening me to real cares;
And yet, a king – though prudence well
Have taught thy subject to rebel.

And am I wrong to worship where
Faith cannot doubt nor Hope despair
Since my own soul can grant my prayer?
Speak, God of Visions, plead for me
And tell why I have chosen thee!

AH! WHY, BECAUSE THE DAZZLING SUN (6)

Ah! why, because the dazzling sun
Restored my earth to joy
Have you departed, every one,
And left a desert sky?

All through the night, your glorious eyes
Were gazing down in mine,
And with a full heart's thankful sighs
I blessed that watch divine!

I was at peace, and drank your beams
As they were life to me
And revelled in my changeful dreams
Like petrel on the sea.

Thought followed thought – star followed star
Through boundless regions on,
While one sweet influence, near and far,
Thrilled through and proved us one.

Why did the morning rise to break
So great, so pure a spell,
And scorch with fire the tranquil cheek
Where your cool radiance fell?

Blood-red he rose, and arrow-straight
His fierce beams struck my brow:
The soul of Nature, sprang elate.
But mine sank sad and low!

My lids closed down – yet through their veil
I saw him blazing still;
And bathe in gold the misty dale,
And flash upon the hill.

I turned me to the pillow then
To call back Night, and see
Your worlds of solemn light, again
Throb with my heart and me!

It would not do – the pillow glowed,
And glowed both roof and floor,
And birds sang loudly in the wood,
And fresh winds shook the door.

The curtains waved, the wakened flies
Were murmuring round my room,
Imprisoned there, till I should rise
And give them leave to roam.

O stars and Dreams and Gentle Night;
O Night and Stars return!
And hide me from the hostile light
That does not warm, but burn –

That drains the blood of suffering men;
Drinks tears, instead of dew:
Let me sleep through his blinding reign,
And only wake with you!

NO COWARD SOUL IS MINE (7)

No coward soul is mine
No trembler in the world's storm-troubled sphere
I see Heaven's glories shine
And Faith shines equal arming me from Fear

O God within my breast
Almighty ever-present Deity
Life, that in me hast rest
As I, Undying Life, have power in Thee

Vain are the thousand creeds
That move men's hearts, unutterably vain,
Worthless as withered weeds
Or idlest froth amid the boundless main

To waken doubt in one
Holding so fast by thy infinity
So surely anchored on
The steadfast rock of Immortality

With wide-embracing love
Thy spirit animates eternal years
Pervades and broods above,
Changes, sustains, dissolves, creates and rears

Though Earth and Moon were gone
And suns and universes ceased to be
And thou wert left alone
Every Existence would exist in thee

There is not room for Death
Nor atom that his might could render void
Since thou art Being and Breath
And what thou art may never be destroyed.

(8) D.G.C. TO J.A.

Come, the wind may never again
Blow as now it blows for us;
And the stars may never again shine as they now shine;
Long before October returns,
Seas of blood will have parted us;
And you must crush the love in your heart, and I the love
in mine!

For face to face will our kindred stand,
And as they are so shall we be;
Forgetting how the same sweet earth has borne and
nourished all –
One must fight for the people's power,
And one for the rights of Royalty;
And each be ready to give his life to work the other's fall.

The chance of war we cannot shun,
Nor would we shrink from our fathers' cause,
Nor dred Death more because the hand that gives it may
be dear;
We must bear to see Ambition rule
Over Love, with his iron laws;
Must yield our blood for a stranger's sake, and refuse
ourselves a tear!

So, the wind may never again
Blow as now it blows for us,
And the stars may never again shine as now they shine;
Next October, the cannon's roar

From hostile ranks may be urging us –
Me to strike for your life's blood, and you to strike for
mine.

From JULIAN M. and A.G. ROCHELLE (9)

Silent is the House – all are laid asleep;
One, alone, looks out o'er the snow wreaths deep;
Watching every cloud, dreading every breeze
That whirls the 'wildering drifts and bends the groaning
trees.

Cheerful is the hearth, soft the matted floor;
Not one shivering gust creeps through pane or door;
The little lamp burns straight, its rays shoot strong and far;
I trim it well to be the Wanderer's guiding-star.

Frown, my haughty sire; chide, my angry dame;
Set your slaves to spy, threaten me with shame:
But neither sire nor dame, nor prying serf shall know
What angel nightly tracks that waste of winter snow.

In the dungeon crypts idly did I stray,
Reckless of the lives wasting there away;
'Draw the ponderous bars; open, Warder stern!'
He dare not say me nay – the hinges harshly turn.

'Our guests are darkly lodged,' I whispered, gazing through
The vault whose grated eye showed Heaven more grey than
blue.
(This was when glad spring laughed in awaking pride.)
'Aye, darkly lodged enough!' returned my sullen guide.

Then, God forgive my youth, forgive my careless tongue!
I scoffed, as the chill chains on the damp flagstones rung;
'Confined in triple walls, art thou so much to fear,
That we must bind thee down and clench thy fetters here?'

The captive raised her face; it was as soft and mild
As sculptured marble saint or slumbering, unweaned child;
It was so soft and mild, it was so sweet and fair,
Pain could not trace a line nor grief a shadow there!

The captive raised her hand and pressed it to her brow;
'I have been struck,' she said, 'and I am suffering now;
Yet these are little worth, your bolts and irons strong;
And were they forged in steel they could not hold me long.'

Hoarse laughed the jailor grim: 'Shall I be won to hear;
Dost think, fond dreaming wretch, that I shall grant thy
prayer?
Or, better still, wil't melt my master's heart with groans?
Ah, sooner might the sun thaw down these granite stones!

'My master's voice is low, his aspect bland and kind,
But hard as hardest flint the soul that lurks behind;
And I am rough and rude, yet not more rough to see
Than is the hidden ghost which has its home in me!'

About her lips there played a smile of almost scorn;
'My friend,' she gently said, 'you have not heard me mourn;
When you my parents' lives – my lost life, can restore,
Then may I weep and sue – but never, Friend, before!'

Her head sank on her hands; its fair curls swept the ground;
The dungeon seemed to swim in strange confusion round –
'Is she so near to death?' I murmured, half aloud,
And, kneeling, parted back the floating golden cloud.

Alas, how former days upon my heart were borne;
How memory mirrored then the prisoner's joyous morn:
Too blithe, too loving child, too warmly, wildly gay!
Was that the wintry close of thy celestial May?

She knew me and she sighed, 'Lord Julian, can it be,
Of all my playmates, you alone remember me?
Nay, start not at my words, unless you deem it shame
To own, from conquered foe, a once familiar name.

'I cannot wonder now at ought the world will do,
And insult and contempt I lightly brook from you,
Since those, who vowed away their souls to win my love,
Around this living grave like utter strangers move!

'Nor has one voice been raised to plead that I might die,
Not buried under earth but in the open sky;
By ball or speedy knife or headsman's skilful blow –
A quick and welcome pang instead of lingering woe!

'Yet, tell them, Julian, all, I am not doomed to wear
Year after year in gloom and desolate despair;
A messenger of Hope comes every night to me,
And offers, for short life, eternal liberty.

'He comes with western winds, with evening's wandering
  airs,
With that clear dusk of heaven that brings the thickest stars;
Winds take a pensive tone, and stars a tender fire,
And visions rise and change which kill me with desire –

'Desire for nothing known in my maturer years
When joy grew mad with awe at counting future tears;
When, if my spirit's sky was full of flashes warm,
I knew not whence they came, from sun or thunderstorm;

'But first a hush of peace, a soundless calm descends;
The struggle of distress and fierce impatience ends;
Mute music soothes my breast – unuttered harmony
That I could never dream till earth was lost to me.

'Then dawns the Invisible, the Unseen its truth reveals;
My outward sense is gone, my inward essence feels –
Its wings are almost free, its home, its harbour found;
Measuring the gulf it stoops and dares the final bound!

'Oh, dreadful is the check – intense the agony
When the ear begins to hear and the eye begins to see;
When the pulse begins to throb, the brain to think again,
The soul to feel the flesh and the flesh to feel the chain!'

(10) R. ALCONA TO J. BRENZAIDA

Cold in the earth, and the deep snow piled above thee!
Far, far removed, cold in the dreary grave!
Have I forgot, my Only Love, to love thee,
Severed at last by Time's all-wearing wave?

Now, when alone, do my thoughts no longer hover
Over the mountains on Angora's shore;
Resting their wings where heath and fern-leaves cover
That noble heart for ever, ever more?

Cold in the earth, and fifteen wild Decembers
From those brown hills have melted into Spring –
Faithful indeed is the spirit that remembers
After such years of change and suffering!

Sweet Love of youth, forgive if I forget thee
While the World's tide is bearing me along:
Sterner desires and darker hopes beset me,
Hopes which obscure but cannot do thee wrong.

No other Sun has lightened up my Heaven;
No other Star has ever shone for me:
All my life's bliss from thy dear life was given –
All my life's bliss is in the grave with thee.

But when the days of golden dreams had perished
And even Despair was powerless to destroy,
Then did I learn how existence could be cherished,
Strengthened and fed without the aid of joy;

Then did I check the tears of useless passion,
Weaned my young soul from yearning after thine;
Sternly denied its burning wish to hasten
Down to that tomb already more than mine!

And even yet, I dare not let it languish,
Dare not indulge in Memory's rapturous pain;
Once drinking deep of that divinest anguish,
How could I seek the empty world again?

THE LINNET IN THE ROCKY DELLS (11)

The linnet in the rocky dells,
The moor-lark in the air,
The bee among the heather-bells
That hide my Lady fair:

The wild deer browse above her breast;
The wild birds raise their brood;
And they, her smiles of love caressed,
Have left her solitude!

I ween, that when the grave's dark wall
Did first her form retain,
They thought their hearts could ne'er recall
The light of joy again.

They thought the tide of grief would flow
Unchecked through future years,
But where is all their anguish now,
And where are all their tears?

Well, let them fight for Honour's breath,
Or Pleasure's shade pursue –
The Dweller in the land of Death
Is changed and careless too.

And if their eyes should watch and weep
Till Sorrow's source were dry,
She would not, in her tranquil sleep,
Return a single sigh.

Blow, west wind, by the lonely mound,
And murmur, summer streams,
There is no need of other sound
To soothe my Lady's dreams.

(12) THE RUNAWAY SLAVE AT PILGRIM'S POINT

I

I stand on the mark beside the shore
Of the first white pilgrim's bended knee,
Where exile turned to ancestor,
And God was thanked for liberty.
I have run through the night, my skin is as dark,
I bend my knee down on this mark:
I look on the sky and the sea.

II

O pilgrim-souls, I speak to you!
I see you come proud and slow
From the land of the spirits pale as dew
And round me and round me ye go.
O pilgrims, I have gasped and run
All night long from the whips of one
Who in your names works sin and woe!

III

And thus I thought that I would come
And kneel here where ye knelt before,
And feel your souls around me hum
In undertone to the ocean's roar;
And lift my black face, my black hand,
Here, in your names, to curse this land
Ye blessed in freedom's, evermore.

IV

I am black, I am black,
And yet God made me, they say:
But if He did so, smiling back
He must have cast his work away
Under the feet of his white creatures,
With a look of scorn, that the dusky features
Might be trodden again to clay.

V

And yet He has made dark things
   To be glad and merry as light:
There's a little dark bird sits and sings,
   There's a dark stream ripples out of
      sight,
And the dark frogs chant in the safe morass,
And the sweetest stars are made to pass
   O'er the face of the darkest night.

VI

But *we* who are dark, we are dark!
   Ah God, we have no stars!
About our souls in care and cark
   Our blackness shuts like prison-bars:
The poor souls crouch so far behind
That never a comfort can they find
   By reaching through the prison-bars.

VII

Indeed we live beneath the sky,
   That great smooth Hand of God stretched out
On all His children fatherly,
   To save them from the dread and doubt
Which would be if, from this low place,
All opened straight up to His face
   Into the grand eternity.

VIII

And still God's sunshine and his frost,
   They make us hot, they make us cold,
As if we were not black and lost;
   And the beasts and the birds, in wood and fold,
Do fear and take us for very men:
Could the whip-or-will or the cat of the glen
   Look into my eyes and be bold?

IX

I am black, I am black!
  But, once, I laughed in girlish glee,
For one of my colour stood in the track
  Where the drivers drove, and looked at me,
And tender and full was the look he gave –
Could a slave look so at another slave? –
  I look at the sky and the sea.

X

And from that hour our spirits grew
  As free as if unsold, unbought:
Oh, strong enough, since we were two,
  To conquer the world, we thought.
The drivers drove us day by day;
We did not mind, we went one way,
  And no better a freedom sought.

XI

In the sunny ground between the canes,
  He said, 'I love you' as he passed;
When the shingle-roof rang fast with the rains,
  I heard how he vowed it fast:
While others shook he smiled in the hut,
As he carved me a bowl of the cocoa-nut
  Through the roar of the hurricanes.

XII

I sang his name instead of a song,
  Over and over I sang his name,
Upward and downward I drew it along
  My various notes, – the same, the same!
I sang it low, that the slave-girls near
Might never guess, from aught they could hear,
  It was only a name – a name.

XIII

I look on the sky and the sea.
  We were two to love and two to pray:

Yes, two, O God, who cried to Thee,
  Though nothing didst Thou say!
Coldly Thou sat'st behind the sun:
And now I cry who am but one,
  Thou wilt not speak to-day.

XIV

We were black, we were black,
  We had no claim to love and bliss,
What marvel if each went to wrack?
  They wrung my cold hands out of his,
They dragged him – where? I crawled to touch
His blood's mark in the dust . . . not much,
  Ye pilgrims' souls, though plain as *this*!

XV

Wrong, followed by a deeper wrong!
  Mere grief's too good for such as I:
So the white men brought the shame ere long
  To strangle the sob of my agony.
They would not leave me for my dull
Wet eyes! – it was too merciful
  To let me weep pure tears and die.

XVI

I am black, I am black!
  I wore a child upon my breast,
An amulet that hung too slack,
  And in my unrest, could not rest:
Thus we went moaning, child and mother
One to another, one to another,
  Until all ended for the best.

VXII

For hark! I will tell you low, low,
  I am black, you see, –
And the babe who lay on my bosom so,
  Was far too white, too white for me;
As white as those ladies who scorned to pray

Beside me at church but yesterday,
   Though my tears had washed a place for
         my knee.

XVIII

My own, own child! I could not bear
   To look in his face, it was so white;
I covered him up with a kerchief there,
   I covered his face in close and tight:
And he moaned and struggled, as well
         might be,
For the white child wanted his liberty –
   Ha, ha! he wanted the master-right.

XIX

He moaned and beat with his head and feet,
   His little feet that never grew;
He struck them out, as it was meet,
   Against my heart to break it through:
I might have sung and made him mild,
But I dared not sing to the white-faced child
   The only song that I knew.

XX

I pulled the kerchief very close:
   He could not see the sun, I swear,
More, then, alive, than now he does
   From between the roots of the mango
         . . . where?
I know where. Close! A child and mother
Do wrong to look at one another
   When one is black and one is fair.

XXI

Why, in that single glance I had
   Of my child's face . . . I tell you all,
I saw a look that made me mad!
   The *master's* look, that used to fall
On my soul like a lash . . . or worse!

And so, to save it from my curse,
  I twisted it round in my shawl.

XXII

And he moaned and trembled from foot to head,
  He shivered from head to foot;
Till after a time he lay instead
  Too suddenly still and mute.
I felt, beside, a stiffening cold:
I dared to lift up just a fold,
  As in lifting a leaf of the mango-fruit.

XXIII

But *my* fruit . . . ha, ha! – there, had been
  (I laugh to think on't at this hour!)
Your fine white angels (who have seen
  Nearest the secret of God's power)
And plucked my fruit to make them wine,
And sucked the soul of that child of mine
  As the humming bird sucks the soul of the flower.

XXIV

Ha, ha, the trick of the angels white!
  They freed the white child's spirit so.
I said not a word, but day and night
  I carried the body to and fro,
And it lay on my heart like a stone, as chill.
– The sun may shine out as much as he will:
  I am cold, though it happened a month ago.

XXV

From the white man's house, and the
    black man's hut,
I carried the little body on:
The forest's arms did round us shut
  And silence through the trees did run:
They asked no question as I went,
They stood too high for astonishment,
  They could see God sit on His throne.

XXVI

My little body, kerchiefed fast,
I bore it on through the forest, on;
And when I felt it was tired at last,
I scooped a hole beneath the moon:
Through the forest-tops the angels far,
With a white sharp finger from every star,
Did point and mock at what was done.

XXVII

Yet when it was all done aright,–
Earth, 'twixt me and my baby, strewed,–
All, changed to black earth,– nothing white,–
A dark child in the dark! – ensued
Some comfort, and my heart grew young;
I sate down smiling there and sung
The song I learnt in my maidenhood.

XXVIII

And thus we two were reconciled,
The white child and black mother, thus;
For as I sang it soft and wild,
The same song, more melodious,
Rose from the grave whereon I sate:
It was the dead child singing that,
To join the souls of both of us.

XXIX

I look on the sea and the sky.
Where the pilgrims' ships first anchored lay
The free sun rideth gloriously,
But the pilgrim ghosts have slid away
Through the earliest streaks of the morn:
My face is black, but it glares with a scorn
Which they dare not meet by day.

XXX

Ha!– in her stead, their hunter sons!
Ha! ha! they are on me – they hunt in a ring!

Keep off! I brave you all at once,
    I throw off your eyes like snakes that sting!
You have killed the black eagle at nest, I think:
Did you ever stand still in your triumph,
            and shrink
    From the stroke of her wounded wing?

XXXI

(Man, drop that stone you dared to lift!—)
    I wish you who stand there five abreast,
Each for his own wife's joy and gift,
    A little corpse as safely at rest
As mine in the mangoes! Yes, but *she*
May keep live babies on her knee,
    And sing the song she likes the best.

XXXII

I am not mad: I am black.
    I see you staring in my face —
I know you staring, shrinking back,
    Ye are born of the Washington-race,
And this land is the free America,
And this mark on my wrist— I prove what I say)
    Ropes tied me up here to the flogging place.

XXXIII

You think I shrieked then? Not a sound.
    I hung, as a gourd hangs in the sun;
I only cursed them all around
    As softly as I might have done
My very own child: from these sands
Up to the mountains, lift your hands,
    O slaves, and end what I begun!

XXXIV

Whips, curses; these must answer those!
    For in this UNION you have set
Two kinds of men in adverse rows,
    Each loathing each; and all forget

The seven wounds in Christ's body fair,
While HE sees gaping everywhere
    Our countless wounds that pay no debt.

XXXV

Our wounds are different. Your white men
    Are after all, not gods indeed,
Nor able to make Christ's again
    Do good with bleeding. *We* who bleed
(Stand off!) we help not in our loss!
We are too heavy for our cross,
    And fall and crush you and your seed.

XXXVI

I fall, I swoon! I look at the sky.
    The clouds are breaking on my brain;
I am floated along, as if I should die
    Of liberty's exquisite pain.
In the name of the white child waiting for me
In the death-dark where we may kiss and agree,
White men, I leave you all curse-free
    In my broken heart's disdain!

(13) TWO SONNETS FROM THE PORTUGUESE

XIII

And wilt thou have me fashion into speech
The love I bear thee, finding words enough,
And hold the torch out, while the winds are rough,
Between our faces, to cast light on each? –
I drop it at thy feet. I cannot teach
My hand to hold my spirit so far off
From myself – me – that I should bring thee proof
In words, of love hid in me out of reach.
Nay, let the silence of my womanhood
Commend my woman-love to thy belief, –

Seeing that I stand unwon, however wooed,
And rend the garment of my life, in brief,
By a most dauntless, voiceless fortitude,
Lest one touch of this heart convey its grief.

XVII

My poet, thou canst touch on all the notes
God set between His After and Before,
And strike up and strike off the general roar
Of the rushing worlds a melody that floats
In a serene air purely. Antidotes
Of medicated music, answering for
Mankind's forlornest uses, thou canst pour
From thence into their ears. God's will devotes
Thine to such ends, and mine to wait on thine.
How, Dearest, wilt thou have me for most use?
A hope, to sing by gladly? or a fine
Sad memory, with thy songs to interfuse?
A shade, in which to sing – of palm or pine?
A grave, on which to rest from singing?
    Choose.

From AURORA LEIGH (14)

A

And I, I was a good child on the whole,
A meek and manageable child. Why not?
I did not live, to have the faults of life:
There seemed more true life in my father's grave
Than in all England. Since that threw me off
Who fain would cleave (his latest Will, they say,
Consigned me to his land), I only thought
Of lying quiet there where I was thrown
Like sea-weed on the rocks, and suffering her
To prick me to a pattern with her pin,

Fibre from fibre, delicate leaf from leaf,
And dry out from my drowned anatomy
The last sea-salt left in me.
                                        So it was.

I broke the copious curls upon my head
In braids, because she liked smooth-ordered hair,
I left off saying my sweet Tuscan words
Which still at any stirring of the heart
Came up to float across the English phrase
As lilies (Bene or Che che), because
She liked my father's child to speak his tongue.
I learnt the collects and the catechism,
The creeds, from Athanasius back to Nice,
The Articles, the Tracts against the times
(By no means Buonaventure's 'Prick of Love'),
And various popular synopses of
Inhuman doctrines never taught by John,
Because she liked instructed piety.
I learnt my complement of classic French
(Kept pure of Balzac and neologism)
And German also, since she liked a range
Of liberal education, – tongues, not books.
I learnt a little algebra, a little
Of the mathematics, – brushed with extreme flounce
The circle of the sciences, because
She misliked women who are frivolous.
I learnt the royal genealogies
Of Oviedo, the internal laws
Of the Burmese empire, – by how many feet
Mount Chimborazo outsoars Teneriffe,
What navigable river joins itself
To Lara, and what census of the year five
Was taken at Klagenfurt, – because she liked
A general insight into useful facts.
I learnt much music, – such as would have been
As quite impossible in Johnson's day

As still it might be wished – fine sleights of hand
And unimagined fingering, shuffling off
The hearer's soul through hurricanes of notes
To a noisy Tophet; and I drew . . . costumes
From French engravings, nereids neatly draped
(With smirks of simmering godship): I washed in
Landscapes from nature (rather say, washed out).
I danced the polka and Cellarius,
Spun glass, stuffed birds, and modelled flowers in wax,
Because she liked accomplishments in girls.
I read a score of books on womanhood
To prove, if women do not think at all,
They may teach thinking (to a maiden aunt
Or else the author), – books that boldy assert
Their right of comprehending husband's talk
When not too deep, and even of answering
With pretty 'may it please you,' or 'so it is,' –
Their rapid insight and fine aptitude,
Particular worth and general missionariness,
As long as they keep quiet by the fire
And never say 'no' when the world says 'ay',
For that is fatal – their angelic reach
Of virtue, chiefly used to sit and darn,
And fatten household sinners, – their, in brief,
Potential faculty in everything
Of abdicating power in it: she owned
She liked a woman to be womanly,
And English women, she thanked God and sighed
(Some people always sigh in thanking God),
Were models to the universe. And last
I learnt cross-stitch, because she did not like
To see me wear the night with empty hands
A-doing nothing. So, my shepherdness
Was something after all (the pastoral saints
Be praised for't), leaning lovelorn with pink eyes
To match her shoes, when I mistook the silks;
Her head uncrushed by that round weight of hat

So strangely similar to the tortoise-shell
Which slew the tragic poet.
                                        By the way,
The works of women are symbolical.
We sew, sew, prick our fingers, dull our sight,
Producing what? A pair of slippers, sir,
To put on when you're weary – or a stool
To stumble over and vex you . . . 'curse that stool!'
Or else at best, a cushion, where you lean
And sleep, and dream of something we are not
But would be for your sake. Alas, alas!
This hurts most, this – that, after all, we are paid
The worth of our work, perhaps.
                                        In looking down
Those years of education (to return)
I wonder if Brinvilliers suffered more
In the water-torture . . . flood succeeding flood.
To drench the incapable throat and split the veins . . .
Than I did. Certain of your feebler souls
Go out in such a process; many pine
To a sick, inodorous light; my own endured:
I had relations in the Unseen, and drew
The elemental nutriment and heat
From nature, as earth feels the sun at nights,
Or as a babe sucks surely in the dark.
I kept the life thrust on me, on the outside
Of the inner life with all its ample room
For heart and lungs, for will and intellect,
Inviolable by conventions. God,
I thank thee for that grace of thine!

B

                                        'There it is! –
You play beside a death-bed like a child,
Yet measure to yourself a prophet's place
To teach the living. None of all these things
Can women understand. You generalise

Oh, nothing, – not even grief! Your quick-breathed hearts,
So sympathetic to the personal pang,
Close on each separate knife-stroke, yielding up
A whole life at each wound, incapable
Of deepening, widening a large lap of life
To hold the world-full woe. The human race
To you means, such a child, or such a man,
You saw one morning waiting in the cold,
Beside that gate perhaps. You gather up
A few such cases, and when strong sometimes
Will write of factories and of slaves, as if
Your father were a negro, and your son
A spinner in the mills. All's yours and you,
All, coloured with your blood, or otherwise
Just nothing to you. Why, I call you hard
To general suffering. Here's the world half-blind
With intellectual light, half-brutalised
With civilisation, having caught the plague
In silks from Tarsus, shrieking east and west
Along a thousand railroads, mad with pain
And sin too! . . . does one woman of you all
(You who weep easily) grow pale to see
This tiger shake his cage? – does one of you
Stand still from dancing, stop from stringing pearls,
And pine and die because of the great sum
Of universal anguish? – Show me a tear
Wet as Cordelia's, in eyes bright as yours,
Because the world is mad. You cannot count,
That you should weep for this account, not you!
You weep for what you know. A red-haired child
Sick in a fever, if you touch him once,
Though but so little as with a finger-tip,
Will set you weeping; but a million sick . . .
You could as soon weep for the rule of three
Or compound fractions. Therefore, this same world,
Uncomprehended by you, must remain
Uninfluenced by you. – Women as you are,

Mere women, personal and passionate,
You give us doating mothers, and perfect wives,
Sublime Madonnas, and enduring saints!
We get no Christ from you, – and verily
We shall not get a poet, in my mind.'
'With which conclusion you conclude'. . .
'But this,'
That you, Aurora, with the large live brow
And steady eyelids, cannot condescend
To play at art, as children play at swords,
To show a pretty spirit, chiefly admired
Because true action is impossible
You never can be satisfied with praise
Which men give women when they judge a book
Not as mere work but as mere woman's work,
Expressing the comparative respect
Which means the absolute scorn. 'Oh, excellent,
What grace, what facile turns, what fluent sweeps,
What delicate discernment . . . almost thought!
The book does honour to the sex, we hold.
Among our female authors we make room
For this fair writer, and congratulate
The country that produces in these times
Such women, competent to . . . spell.'
'Stop there,'
I answered, burning through his thread of talk
With a quick flame of emotion, – 'You have read
My soul, if not my book, and argue well
I would not condescend . . . we will not say
To such a kind of praise (a worthless end
Is praise of all kinds) but to such a use
Of holy art and golden life. I am young,
And peradventure weak – you tell me so –
Through being a woman. And, for all the rest,
Take thanks for justice. I would rather dance
At fairs on tight-rope, till the babies dropped
Their gingerbread for joy, – than shift the types

For tolerable verse, intolerable
To men who act and suffer. Better far
Pursue a frivolous trade by serious means,
Than a sublime art frivolously.'

BIANCA AMONG THE NIGHTINGALES (15)

I

The cypress stood up like a church
  That night we felt our love would hold,
And saintly moonlight seemed to search
  And wash the whole world clean gold;
The olives crystallised the vales'
  Broad slopes until the hills grew strong:
The fire-flies and the nightgales
  Throbbed each to either, flame and song,
The nightingales, the nightingales!

II

Upon the angle of its shade
  The cypress stood, self-balanced high;
Half up, half down, as double-made,
  Along the ground, against the sky;
And we, too! from such soul-height went
  Such leaps of blood, so blindly driven,
We scarce knew if our nature meant
  Most passionate earth or intense heaven.
The nightingales, the nightingales!

III

We paled with love, we shook with love,
  We kissed so close we could not vow;
Till Giulio whispered, 'Sweet, above
  God's Ever guaranties this Now.'
And through his words the nightingales
  Drove straight and full their long clear call,

Like arrows through heroic mails,
   And love was aweful in it all.
The nightingales, the nightingales!

IV

O cold white moonlight of the north,
   Refresh these pulses, quench this hell!
O coverture of death drawn forth
   Across this garden-chamber . . . well!
But what have nightingales to do
   In gloomy England, called the free . . .
(Yes, free to die in! . . .) when we two
   Are sundered, singing still to me?
And still they sing, the nightingales!

V

I think I hear him, how he cried
   'My own soul's life!' between their notes.
Each man has but one soul supplied,
   And that's immortal. Though his throat's
On fire with passion now, to her
   He can't say what to me he said!
And yet he moves her, they aver,
   The nightingales sing through my head –
The nightingales, the nightingales!

VI

He says to her what moves her most.
   He would not name his soul within
Her hearing, – rather pays her cost
   With praises to her lips and chin.
Man has but one soul, 'tis ordained,
   And each soul but one love, I add;
Yet souls are damned and love's profaned;
   These nightingales will sing me mad!
The nightingales, the nightingales!

VII

I marvel how the birds can sing,
   There's little difference, in their view,
Betwixt our Tuscan trees that spring
   As vital flames into the blue,
And dull round blots of foliage meant,
   Like saturated sponges here
To suck the fogs up. As content
   Is he too in this land, 'tis clear.
And still they sing, the nightingales.

VIII

My native Florence! dear, foregone!
   I see across the Alpine ridge
How the last feast day of Saint John
   Shot rockets from Carraia bridge.
The luminous city, tall with fire,
   Trod deep down in that river of ours,
While many a boat with lamp and choir
   Skimmed birdlike over glittering towers
I will not hear these nightingales.

IX

I seem to float, we seem to float
   Down Arno's stream in festive guise;
A boat strikes flame into our boat,
   And up that lady seems to rise
As then she rose. The shock had flashed
   A vision on us! What a head,
What leaping eyeballs! – beauty dashed
   To splendour by a sudden dread.
And still they sing, the nightingales.

X

Too bold to sin, too weak to die;
   Such women are so. As for me,
I would we had drowned there, he and I,
   That moment, loving perfectly.

He had not caught her with her loosed
   Gold ringlets . . . rarer in the south . . .
Nor heard the 'Grazie tanto' bruised
   To sweetness by her English mouth.
And still they sing, the nightingales.

XI

She had not reached him at my heart
   With her fine tongue, as snakes indeed
Kill flies; not had I, for my part,
   Yearned after, in my desperate need,
And followed him as he did her
   To coasts left bitter by the tide,
Whose very nightingales, elsewhere
   Delighting, torture and deride!
For still they sing, the nightingales.

XII

A worthless woman; mere cold clay
   As all false things are: but so fair,
She takes the breath of men away
   Who gaze upon her unaware.
I would not play her larcenous tricks
   To have her looks! She lied and stole,
And spat into my love's pure pyx
   The rank saliva of her soul.
And still they sing, the nightingales.

XIII

I would not for her white and pink,
   Though such he likes – her grace of limb,
Though such he has praised – nor yet, I think
   For life itself, though spent with him,
Commit such sacrilege, affront
   God's nature which is love, intrude
'Twixt two affianced souls, and hunt
   Like spiders, in the altar's wood.
I cannot hear these nightingales.

XIV

If she chose sin, some gentler guise
   She might have sinned in, so it seems:
She might have pricked out both my eyes,
   And I still seen him in my dreams!
– Or drugged me in my soup or wine,
   Nor left me angry afterward:
To die here with his hand in mine,
   His breath upon me, were not hard.
(Our Lady hush these nightingales!)

XV

But set a springe for him, 'mio ben,'
   My only good, my first last love!
Though Christ knows well what sin is, when
   He sees some things done they must move
Himself to wonder. Let her pass.
   I think of her by night and day.
Must I too join her . . . out, alas!. . .
   With Giulio, in each word I say?
And evermore the nightingales!

XXVI

Giulio, my Giulio! – sing they so,
   And you be silent? Do I speak,
And you not hear? An arm you throw
   Round someone, and I feel so weak?
– Oh, owl-like birds! They sing for spite,
   They sing for hate, they sing for doom.
They'll sing through death who sing through night,
   They'll sing and stun me in the tomb –
The nightingales, the nightingales!

(16) *From* GOBLIN MARKET

Laughed every goblin
When they spied her peeping:
Came towards her hobbling
Flying, running, leaping,
Puffing and blowing,
Chuckling, clapping, crowing,
Clucking and gobbling,
Mopping and mowing,
Full of airs and graces,
Pulling wry faces,
Demure grimaces,
Cat-like and rat-like,
Ratel and wombat-like,
Snail-paced in a hurry,
Parrot-voiced and whistler,
Helter-skelter, hurry-skurry;
Chattering like magpies,
Fluttering like pigeons,
Gliding like fishes, –
Hugged and kissed her;
Squeezed and caressed her;
Stretched up their dishes,
Panniers and plates:
'Look at our apples
Russet and dun,
Bob at our cherries,
Bite at our peaches,
Citrons and dates,
Grapes for the asking,
Pears red with basking
Out in the sun,
Plums on their twigs;
Pluck them and suck them,
Pomegranates, figs.'

'Good folk,' said Lizzie,
Mindful of Jeanie,
'Give me much and many'; –
Held out her apron,
Tossed them her penny.
'Nay take a seat with us,
Honour and eat with us,'
They answered grinning:
'Our feast is but beginning.
Night yet is early,
Warm and dew pearly,
Wakeful and starry:
Such fruits as these
No man can carry;
Half their bloom would fly,
Half their dew would dry,
Half their flavour would pass by.
Sit down and feast with us,
Be welcome guest with us,
Cheer you and rest with us.'
'Thank you,' said Lizzie, 'but one waits
At home alone for me:
So, without further parleying,
If you will not sell me any
Of your fruits though much and many,
Give me back my silver penny
I tossed you for a fee.'
They began to scratch their pates,
No longer wagging, purring,
But visibly demurring,
Grunting and snarling.
One called her proud,
Cross-grained, uncivil;
Their tones waxed loud,
Their looks were evil.
Lashing their tails
They trod and hustled her,

Elbowed and jostled her,
Clawed with their nails,
Barking, mewing, hissing, mocking,
Tore her gown and soiled her stocking,
Twitched her hair out by the roots,
Stamped upon her tender feet,
Held her hands and squeezed their fruits
Against her mouth to make her eat.

White and golden Lizzie stood,
Like a lily in a flood, –
Like a rock of blue-veined stone
Lashed by tides obstreperously, –
Like a beacon left alone
In a hoary roaring sea,
Sending up a golden fire, –
Like a fruit-crowned orange tree
White with blossoms honey-sweet
Sore beset by wasp and bee –
Like a royal virgin town
Topped with gilded dome and spire
Close beleaguered by a fleet
Mad to tug her standard down.

. . .

She cried, 'Laura' up the garden,
'Did you miss me?
Come and kiss me.
Never mind my bruises
Hug me, kiss me, suck my juices
Squeezed from goblin fruits for you,
Goblin pulp and goblin dew.
Eat me, drink me, love me;
Laura, make much of me:
For your sake I have braved the glen
And had to do with goblin merchant men.'

Laura started from her chair,
Flung her arms up in the air,
Clutched her hair:
'Lizzie, Lizzie, have you tasted
For my sake the fruit forbidden?
Must your light like mine be hidden,
Your young life like mine be wasted,
Undone in mine undoing
And ruined in my ruin,
Thirsty, cankered, goblin ridden?'
She clung about her sister,
Kissed and kissed and kissed her:
Tears once again
Refreshed her shrunken eyes,
Dropping like rain
After long sultry drouth;
Shaking with anguish fear and pain,
She kissed and kissed her with a hungry mouth.

Her lips began to scorch,
That juice was wormwood to her tongue,
She loathed the feast:
Writhing as one possessed she leaped and sung,
Rent all her robe and wrung
Her hands in lamentable haste,
And beat her breast.
Her locks streamed like the torch
Borne by a racer at full speed,
Or like the mane of horses in their flight,
Or like an eagle when she stems the light
Straight towards the sun,
Or like a caged thing freed,
Or like a flying flag when armies run.

Swift fire spread through her veins, knocked at her heart,
Met the fire smouldering there
And overbore its lesser flame;
She gorged on bitterness without a name:

Ah! fool, to choose such part
Of soul-consuming care!
Sense failed in the mortal strife:
Like the watch-tower of a town
Which an earth-quake shatters down,
Like a lightning stricken mast,
Like a wind-uprooted tree
Spun about,
Like a foam topped water-spout
Cast down headlong in the sea,
She fell at last;
Pleasure past and anguish past,
Is it death or is it life?

(17) DREAM-LAND

Where sunless rivers weep
Their waves into the deep,
She sleeps a charmed sleep:
  Awake her not.
Led by a single star,
She came from very far
To seek where shadows are
  Her pleasant lot.

She left the rosy morn,
She left the fields of corn,
For twilight cold and lorn
  And water springs.
Thro' sleep, as thro' a veil,
She sees the sky look pale,
And hears the nightingale
  That sadly sings.

Rest, rest, a perfect rest
Shed over brow and breast;

Her face is toward the west,
   The purple land.
She cannot see the grain
Ripening on hill and plain;
She cannot feel the rain
   Upon her hand.

Rest, rest, for evermore
Upon a mossy shore;
Rest, rest at the heart's core
   Till time shall cease:
Sleep that no pain shall wake;
Night that no morn shall break,
Till joy shall overtake
   Her perfect peace.

MY DREAM (18)

Hear now a curious dream I dreamed last night,
Each word whereof is weighed and sifted truth.

I stood beside Euphrates while it swelled
Like overflowing Jordan in its youth:
It waxed and coloured sensibly to sight,
Till out of myriad pregnant waves there welled
Young crocodiles, a gaunt blunt-featured crew,
Fresh-hatched perhaps and daubed with birthday dew.
The rest if I should tell, I fear my friend,
My closest friend would deem the facts untrue;
And therefore it were wisely left untold;
Yet if you will, why, hear it out to the end.

Each crocodile was girt with massive gold
And polished stones that with their wearers grew:
But one there was who waxed beyond the rest,
Wore kinglier girdle and a kingly crown,
Whilst crowns and orbs and sceptres starred his breast.

All gleamed compact and green with scale on scale,
But special burnishment adorned his mail
And special terror weighed upon his frown;
His punier brethren quaked before his tail,
Broad as a rafter, potent as a flail.
So he grew lord and master of his kin:
But who shall tell the tale of all their woes?
An execrable appetite arose,
He battened on them, crunched, and sucked them in.
He knew no law, he feared no binding law,
But ground them with inexorable jaw:
The luscious fat distilled upon his chin,
Exuded from his nostrils and his eyes,
While still like hungry death he fed his maw;
Till every minor crocodile being dead
And buried too, himself gorged to the full,
He slept with breath oppressed and unstrung claw.
Oh marvel passing strange which next I saw:
In sleep he dwindled to the common size,
And all the empire faded from his coat.
Then from far off a winged vessel came,
Swift as a swallow, subtle as a flame:
I know not what it bore of freight or host,
But white it was as an avenging ghost.
It levelled strong Euphrates in its course;
Supreme yet weightless as an idle mote
It seemed to tame the waters without force
Till not a murmur swelled or billow beat:
Lo, as the purple shadow swept the sands,
The prudent crocodile rose on his feet
And shed appropriate tears and wrung his hands.

What can it mean? you ask. I answer not
For meaning, but myself must echo, What?
And tell it as I saw it on the spot.

WINTER: MY SECRET (19)

I tell my secret? No indeed, not I:
Perhaps some day, who knows?
But not today; it froze, and blows, and snows,
And you're too curious: fie!
You want to hear it? well:
Only, my secret's mine, and I won't tell.

Or, after all, perhaps there's none:
Suppose there is no secret after all,
But only just my fun.
Today's a nipping day, a biting day;
In which one wants a shawl,
A veil, a cloak, and other wraps:
I cannot ope to every one who taps,
And let the draughts come whistling thro' my hall;
Come bounding and surrounding me,
Come buffeting, astounding me,
Nipping and clipping thro' my wraps and all.
I wear my mask for warmth: who ever shows
His nose to Russian snows
To be pecked at by every wind that blows?
You would not peck? I thank you for good will,
Believe, but leave that truth untested still.

Spring's an expansive time: yet I don't trust
March with its peck of dust,
Nor April with its rainbow-crowned brief showers,
Nor even May, whose flowers
One frost may wither thro' the sunless hours.

Perhaps some languid summer day,
When drowsy birds sing less and less,
And golden fruit is ripening to excess,
If there's not too much sun nor too much cloud,
And the warm wind is neither still nor loud,
Perhaps my secret I may say,
Or you may guess.

(20) AUTUMN

I dwell alone – I dwell alone, alone,
Whilst full my river flows down to the sea,
  Gilded with flashing boats
    That bring no friend to me:
O love-songs, gurgling from a hundred throats,
    O love-pangs, let me be.

Fair fall the freighted boats which gold and stone
    And spices bear to sea:
Slim, gleaming maidens swell their mellow notes,
    Love-promising, entreating –
    Ah! sweet, but fleeting –
  Beneath the shivering, snow-white sails.
Hush! the wind flags and fails –

Hush! they will lie becalmed in sight of strand –
  Sight of my strand, where I do dwell alone;
Their songs wake singing echoes in my land –
  They cannot hear me moan.

  One latest, solitary swallow flies
  Across the sea, rough autumn-tempest tost,
  Poor bird, shall it be lost?
Dropped down into this uncongenial sea,
    With no kind eyes
    To watch it while it dies,
  Unguessed, uncared for, free:
    Set free at last,
    The short pang past,
In sleep, in death, in dreamless sleep locked fast.

Mine avenue is all a growth of oaks,
    Some rent by thunder-strokes,
Some rustling leaves and acorns in the breeze;
    Fair fall my fertile trees,
That rear their goodly heads, and live at ease.

A spider's web blocks all mine avenue;
He catches down and foolish painted flies,
That spider wary and wise.
Each morn it hangs a rainbow strung with dew
Betwixt boughs green with sap,
So fair, few creatures guess it is a trap:
I will not mar the web,
Tho' sad I am to see the small lives ebb.

It shakes – my trees shake – for a wind is roused
In cavern where it housed:
Each white and quivering sail,
Of boats among the water leaves
Hollows and strains in the full-throated gale:
Each maiden sings again –
Each languid maiden, whom the calm
Had lulled to sleep with rest and spice and balm.
Miles down my river to the sea
They float and wane,
Long miles away from me.
Perhaps they say: 'She grieves,
Uplifted, like a beacon, on her tower.'
Perhaps they say: 'One hour
More, and we dance among the golden sheaves.'
Perhaps they say: 'One hour
More, and we stand,
Face to face, hand in hand;
Make haste, O slack gale, to the looked-for land!'

My trees are not in flower,
I have no bower,
And gusty creaks my tower,
And lonesome, very lonesome, is my strand.

(21) A ROYAL PRINCESS

I, a princess, king-descended, decked with jewels, gilded,
drest,
Would rather be a peasant with her baby at her breast,
For all I shine so like the sun, and am purple like the west.

Two and two my guards behind, two and two before,
Two and two on either hand, they guard me evermore;
Me, poor dove that must not coo-eagle that must not soar.

All my fountains cast up perfumes, all my gardens grow
Scented woods and foreign spices, with all flowers in blow
That are costly, out of season as the seasons go.

All my walls are lost in mirrors, whereupon I trace
Self to right hand, self to left hand, self in every place,
Self-same solitary figure, self-same seeking face.

Then I have an ivory chair high to sit upon,
Almost like my father's chair, which is an ivory throne;
There I sit uplift and upright, there I sit alone.

Alone by day, alone by night, alone days without end;
My father and my mother give me treasure, search and
spend –
O my father! O my mother! have you ne'er a friend?

As I am a lofty princess, so my father is
A lofty king, accomplished in all kingly subtlities
Holding in his strong right hand world-kingdoms' balances.

He has quarrelled with his neighbours, he has scourged his
foes;
Vassal counts and princes follow where his pennon goes,
Long-descended valiant lords whom the vulture knows,

On whose track the vulture swoops, when they ride in
state
To break the strength of armies and topple down the great:
Each of these my courteous servant, none of these my
mate.

My father counting up his strength sets down with equal
pen
So many head of cattle, head of horses, head of men;
These for slaughter, these for labour, with the how and
when.

Some to work on roads, canals; some to man his ships;
Some to smart in mines beneath sharp overseers' whips;
Some to trap fur-beasts in lands where utmost winter nips.

Once it came into my heart and whelmed me like a flood,
That these too are men and women, human flesh and
blood;
Men with hearts and men with souls, tho' trodden down
like mud.

Our feasting was not glad that night, our music was not
gay;
On my mother's graceful head I marked a thread of grey,
My father frowning at the fare seemed every dish to weigh.

I sat beside them sole princess in my exalted place,
My ladies and my gentlemen stood by me on the dais:
A mirror showed me I look old and haggard in the face:

It showed me that my ladies all are fair to gaze upon,
Plump, plenteous-haired, to every one love's secret lore is
known,
They laugh by day, they sleep by night; ah, me, what is a
throne?

The singing men and women sang that night as usual,
The dancers danced in pairs and sets, but music had a fall,
A melancholy windy fall as at a funeral.

Amid the toss of torches to my chamber back we swept;
My ladies loosed my golden chain; meantime I could have
wept
To think of some in galling chains whether they waked or
slept.

I took my bath of scented milk, delicately waited on,
They burned sweet things for my delight, cedar and
cinnamon,
They lit my shaded silver lamp, and left me there alone.

A day went by, a week went by. One day I heard it said:
'Men are clamouring, women, children, clamouring to be
fed;
Men like famished dogs are howling in the streets for
bread.'

So two whispered by my door, not thinking I could hear,
Vulgar naked truth, ungarnished for a royal ear;
Fit for cooping in the background, not to stalk so near.

But I strained my utmost sense to catch this truth, and
mark:
'There are families out grazing like cattle in the park.'
'A pair of peasants must be saved, even if we build an ark.'

A merry jest, a merry laugh, each strolled upon his way;
One was my page, a lad I reared and bore with day by day;
One was my youngest maid, as sweet and white as cream in
May.

Other footsteps followed softly with a weightier tramp;
Voices said: 'Picked soldiers have been summoned from
the camp,
To quell these base-born ruffians who make free to howl
and stamp.'

'Howl and stamp?' one answered: 'They made free to hurl
a stone
At the minister's state coach, well aimed and stoutly
thrown.'
'There's work then for the soldiers, for this rank crop must
be mown.'

'One I saw, a poor old fool with ashes on his head,
Whimpering because a girl had snatched his crust of bread:
Then he dropped; when someone raised him, it turned out
   he was dead.'

'After us the deluge,' was retorted with a laugh:
'If bread's the staff of life, they must walk without a staff.'
'While I've a loaf they're welcome to my blessing and the
   chaff.'

These passed. 'The king:' stand up. Said my father with a
   smile:
'Daughter mine, your mother comes to sit with you
   awhile,
She's sad today, and who but you her sadness can beguile?'

He too left me. Shall I touch my harp now while I wait, –
(I hear them doubling guard below before our palace
   gate) –
Or shall I work the last gold stitch into my veil of state;

Or shall my woman stand and read some unimpassioned
   scene,
There's music of a lulling sort in words that pause
   between;
Or shall she merely fan me while I wait here for the queen?

Again I caught my father's voice in sharp word of
   command:
'Charge!' a clash of steel: 'Charge again, the rebels stand.
Smite and spare not, hand to hand; smite and spare not,
   hand to hand.'

There swelled a tumult at the gate, high voices waxing
   higher;
A flash of red reflected light lit the cathedral spire;
I heard a cry for faggots, then I heard a yell for fire.

'Sit and roast there with your meat, sit and bake there
with your bread,
You who sat to see us starve,' one shrieking woman said:
'Sit on your throne and roast with your crown upon your
head.'

Nay, this thing I will do, while my mother tarrieth,
I will take my fine spun gold, but not to sew therewith,
I will take my gold and gems, and rainbow fan and wreath:

With a ransom in my lap, a king's ransom in my hand,
I will go down to this people, will stand face to face, will
stand
Where they curse king, queen, and princess of this cursed
land.

They shall take all to buy them bread, take all I have to
give;
I, if I perish, perish; they today shall eat and live;
I, if I perish, perish; that's the goal I half conceive:

Once to speak before the world, rend bare my heart and
show
The lesson I have learned, which is death, is life, to know.
I, if I perish, perish; in the name of God I go.

A Vaster Knowledge
WOMEN'S POETRY 1860–1920

Introduction

But I say all the fault's with God himself
who puts too many women in the world.
We ought to die off reasonably and leave
as many as the men want, none to waste.
Augusta Webster (22)

I could see,
Framed by the arbour foliage, which the sun
In setting softly gilded with rich gold,
Those upturned faces, and those placid limbs:
Saw Plato's narrow eyes and niggard mouth,
Which half did smile and half did criticise,
One hand held up, the shapely fingers framed
To gesture of entreaty – 'Hush, I pray,
Do not disturb her; let us hear the rest;
Follow her mood, for here's another phase
Of your black-browed Xantippe . . .'
Amy Levy (24)

So he opes a vaster knowledge to the view,
Love points the way and woman holds the clue;
Elizabeth Wolstenholme-Elmy (28)

I think that my soul is red
Like the soul of a sword or a scarlet flower:
But when these are dead
They have had their hour.
Charlotte Mew (37)

And while this rose made round her cup
The armies died convulsed . . .
Alice Meynell (38)

In *Aurora Leigh* Romney Leigh sums up women – and their writing – as 'mere women, personal and passionate'. It is a belief that many still hold today. All the writers in this section – except possibly Charlotte Mew – had a strong awareness of what was then called the 'woman question' and of its real significance. They wish to take the 'mere' out of 'mere' women and go beyond the 'personal and passionate'.

Nowadays, we might call them 'feminists', though that term was not used until the very end of the nineteenth century, and not much then. Nevertheless, they had a vision of a better life for women which makes them kin to those campaigning for women's rights today. As well as the best known cause – the Vote, they concerned themselves with education and professional opportunities for women, the age of consent, the position of women within marriage and outside it, sexuality, contraception and venereal disease (in an age before effective contraception or antibiotics one of the alternatives to sexual subjugation was celibacy). For a taste of how they experienced these issues, we turn to their writings.

Three things stand out: firstly, intense anger at wrongs done to women; secondly, a romantic vision of how things might be when all dreams have come true; finally, the pride in being one with a movement that is fighting for all women. 'For it is the grandest movement the world has ever seen/ And we'll win the Vote for Women, wearing purple, white and green' (29).

Anger, vision and unity; these reach beyond the nineteenth century: it may not be too difficult for us to appreciate what it was like to experience them then.

There is much anger in the poems that follow; but I believe there is also the idea that anger, itself, can be, in certain circumstances, an achievement of real worth. Anger brings awareness, awareness brings articulacy, which brings speech, and the next step is action. In creating the poem, or the song, the poet finds a voice for her deepest concerns, concerns she might not even have known she had, at least not in the way they emerge through the poem. The process of becoming self-aware, of discovering aspects of yourself that seem new, is part of the process of creating a poem.

Expressing anger at the wrongs done to women can be creative – this is one message the Victorian campaigners sent us across a century, and it is a relevant one. But before we can express anger, fear has to be overcome; and the suffragette songs and poems included in this section of the poetry collection have something to tell us about overcoming the resistances to taking constructive action.

Sometimes that difficulty in taking action – getting a job, joining a political party, joining a church, becoming involved in a campaign, becoming a feminist and so forth, is glossed over. The fear of becoming visible by one's choices is a very real barrier. In some suffragette songs we find exhortations to overcome fears that were obviously very real to many women. 'Long, long, we in the past,/ Cowered in dread from the light of Heaven' (33) – but now, 'in the blaze of day', with 'sight new given' it is impossible that women should not go forward.

Of course anger at injustice may simply serve to create a more firmly entrenched opposition. But anger, by releasing a creative energy, may help to create a context for people to work to make a better world.

The goals of the women's rights campaigners of the Victorian and Edwardian eras were often concrete and specific enough. They envisaged clear and definite reforms in women's employment and education, in women's health issues and in the legal system as it affected women. This may seem realistic enough today, but there was another aspect. In their literature we find Utopian visions of how life will be when all battles have been won – visions, which, depending on your point of view, will seem either embarrassingly naive or wildly daring. They may be summarised as follows: holy celibacy, holy marriage, and holy learning. Holy celibacy concerns visions of societies without men; holy marriage concerns the marriage relationship elevated in spirit to something egalitarian and noble; and, thanks to holy learning, women may move joyfully into research in all branches of the arts and sciences and raise the whole tone of Western civilisation itself.

These visions (the titles are mine) also reveal to us something of the world in which the women's rights campaigners of that period lived. There are certain parallels between what those women did and what those working for women's rights are doing today; but there are substantial differences as well.

Celibacy was certainly understandable as a positive option for the advanced nineteenth-century woman. Contraception was then neither widely available nor especially effective; the 'double standard' (the toleration of male non-monogamy and the fierce condemnation of all female sexual adventures) meant that even the most virtuous wife ran the risk of contracting venereal disease from her husband for which there was no effective cure. Celibacy protected a woman against many things.

Nineteenth-century fiction and poetry include a number of feminist Utopias which depict a world without men. *Herland*, the novel by Charlotte Perkins Gilman, the American economist and feminist, has recently been reprinted; another work in the same spirit is Mary Elizabeth Coleridge's poem, 'The White Women'. White is intended to suggest purity and nobility of spirit. The white women have never been tamed and have always dwelt without men; they are strong, powerful and skilful. They talk with the voice of nature herself:

Their words are not as ours. If a man might go
    Among the waves of Ocean when they break
And hear them – hear the language of the snow
Falling on torrents – he might also know
    The tongue they speak.

Yet however poignant this vision of an alternative existence, a separatist way of life is never put forward as a serious option. The Amazon vision stands more as a symbol for women's true inner nobility (no 'mere' women these) which will surely be valued some day. We hear somewhat more of a vision of the elevation of marriage to something egalitarian and humane. Such a vision satisfies social proprieties and stealthily implies some of the benefits of egalitarian social relationships in general. 'Ellis Ethelmer' (pseudonym of Elizabeth Wolstenholme-Elmy) writes in 'Women Free' (28) of:

'Marriage, which might have been a mateship sweet,/ Where equal souls in hallowed converse meet,/ Each aiding each the higher truths to find,/ And raising body to the plane of mind' (28).

However, the real way forward is through learning and gaining knowledge and skills. In her grandiose conclusion she sings the praises of 'Earth's advancing queen' and encourages her to find the 'potency divine' that lies burried deep within her, sleeping in her heart. But woman needs to waken her own sleeping princess.

> Woman's own soul must seek and find that fay,
> And wake it into light of quickening day;
> . . . [Man's] philosophic and chirurgic lore,
> To her imparted swell her innate store,
> Till clothed with majesty of mind she stand,
> Regent of Nature's will, in heart, in head, in hand.

The phrase 'majesty of mind' must have had a fine ring to women of the nineteenth century, beginning as they were to free themselves from the oppression of inadequate education and prejudice, and to struggle for a life where they could make a greater contribution to their world, both private and public, and find a greater sense of fulfilment in the process.

NOTE

In order to preserve as nearly as possible the original line breaks, the poems of Charlotte Mew have been set in a smaller typesize.

The Poets

AUGUSTA WEBSTER 1837–94 (22) (23). Augusta Webster was born in Poole, Dorset, the daughter of a vice-admiral and educated at the Cambridge School of Art and in France. In December 1863 she married Thomas Webster, Fellow and subsequently Lecturer in Law at Trinity College, Cambridge. They had one daughter. From 1870 onwards she lived in London. She wrote poetry and plays and was the author of notable translations from the Greek; she also campaigned for women's rights in education and employment. Her dramatic monologue 'The Castaway' which appeared in *Portraits*, published in 1870, created a sensation because of its outspoken social criticism. In her day Augusta Webster had quite a reputation as a thinker and social commentator and contemporary criticism had a hard time equating this with her sex. She died at Kew at the age of fifty-seven.

AMY LEVY 1861–89 (24). Amy Levy was born in Clapham, the daughter of an editor. The family moved from London to Brighton in 1876. Amy grew up and was educated in Brighton and then Newnham College, Cambridge. She wrote poetry from childhood. 'Xantippe' is taken from her first book of poems, *Xantippe*, published in 1881. I have reproduced it here because it suggests something of what the academic establishment must have looked like to a woman – see Xantippe trying to break in on Socrates' conversation to put her point of view without following the formal rules of debate (24). Her later life is uncertain: some say she worked in a factory, some as a teacher in London. In 1889 her second volume of poems, *A London Plane Tree*, was published and her controversial novel of Jewish life *Reuben Sachs Ahad* appeared in 1888. In 1889 she committed suicide by suffocating herself with charcoal fumes. The coroner recorded a verdict of 'self destruction. . . cause unknown'.

MARY ELIZABETH COLERIDGE 1861–1907 (25) (26) (27). Mary Elizabeth Coleridge was a poet, novelist and critic. Her father's grandfather was an elder brother of Samuel Taylor Coleridge. She was born in London and educated at home. Though born to a life of privilege, reading Tolstoy had awakened in her a desire to help the poor. She taught working women at her home and, from 1895 to 1907, at the Working Women's College. Her mother died in 1898 and she continued to live with her father and sister, dying after a sudden illness at Harrogate in August 1907. See *Collected Poems* (1954).

ELIZABETH WOLSTENHOLME-ELMY 1834–1918 (28). Elizabeth Wolstenholme-Elmy was a life-long progressive and campaigner for women's rights who joined the suffrage struggle in her seventies. She wrote outspoken books about married love under the pen-name

'Ellis Ethelmer', and also 'Woman Free', two extracts of which are reproduced below. 'Woman Free' is a sixty-three-stanza poem followed by 200 pages of notes. The author's purpose is to throw the weight of Victorian progressive opinion behind the question of rights for women.

WOMEN'S SOCIAL AND POLITICAL UNION (29) (32) (33). The W.S.P.U. was founded in Manchester in 1904. Initially one of many suffrage societies, the W.S.P.U. gained prominence through militant tactics, charismatic leadership and efficient organisation. 'The Women's Marseillaise' and 'March of the Women' were the militant suffrage movement's two best known anthems. Cicely Hamilton (1872–1952), playwright, novelist and author of *Marriage as a Trade*, wrote the 'March' in 1911 and Ethel Smyth (1858–1944), a fine composer, militant suffragette and friend of Emmeline Pankhurst, wrote the music. Unfortunately no biographical information was available on L.E. Morgan-Browne, Christina Walsh or F.E.M. Macaulay.

CHARLOTTE MEW 1870–1928 (34) (35) (36) (37). Charlotte Mew was born in London the daughter of Frederick Mew, an architect, and Anne Kendall Mew. She was educated privately at the Lucy Harrison School for Girls, Gower Street. Overwhelmed by ill health, family death and poverty, she had a poor opinion of her self and her writing. Her output was small but extraordinary (see *Collected Poems and Prose*, 1981). She was awarded a Civil List Pension on the recommendation of Thomas Hardy, John Masefield and Walter de la Mare. She was a petite, eccentric-looking woman, appearing in masculine clothes at Harold and Alida Monro's poetry bookshop where poets regularly met. She committed suicide.

ALICE MEYNELL 1847–1922 (38) (39) (40) (41). Alice Meynell was well known in her day as a poet and essayist. Her father was a man of wealth and culture but no profession; her mother was a concert pianist. Alice and her sister Elizabeth were educated by their father in a roving life that took them through France, Switzerland, England and Italy. Alice was converted to Catholicism at the age of twenty and in 1875 her first volume of poems was published. She was friendly with the great writers of her time – including Coventry Patmore, George Meredith and Francis Thompson. It was through Francis Thompson that she met the Catholic journalist and literary critic, Wilfred Meynell, whom she married in 1877. Their marriage was very happy and they had eight children. They survived financially by freelance journalism. Alice Meynell wrote many magazine articles which, though fairly hastily written, were of enduring worth and many of them were later collected and published in book form. In spite of the constant demands of a large family, Alice Meynell maintained a deep interest in contemporary social issues and endeavours and supported many humanitarian projects, including the women's suffage campaign. She liked to describe herself as a Christian socialist and feminist in 'lawful and dignified ways'. She is represented here by a small selection of her war poetry, which she considered among her greatest achievements.

Augusta Webster

From A CASTAWAY (22)

Well, well, I know the wise ones talk and talk;
'here's cause, here's cure:' 'No here it is and here:'
and find society to blame, or law,
the Church, the men, the women, too few schools
too many schools, too much, too little taught:
somewhere or somehow someone is to blame:
but I say all the fault's with God himself
who puts too many women in the world.
We ought to die off reasonably and leave
as many as the men want, none to waste.
Here's cause; the woman's superfluity:
and for the cure, why, if it were the law,
say every year, in due percentages,
balancing them with men as the times need,
to kill off female infants, 'twould make room;
and some of us would not have lost too much,
losing life ere we know what it *can* mean.

The other day I saw a woman weep
behind her dead child's bed: the little thing
lay smiling, and the mother wailed half mad,
shrieking to God to give it back again.
I could have laughed aloud: the little girl
living but had her mother's life to live;
there she lay smiling, and her mother wept
to know her gone!
My mother would have wept.

Oh mother, mother, did you ever dream,
you good grave simple mother, you pure soul
no evil could come nigh, did you once dream
in all your dying cares for your lone girl
left to fight out her fortune all alone
that there would be *this* danger? – for *your* girl,
taught by you, lapped in a sweet ignorance,
scarcely more wise of what things sin could be
than some young child a summer six months old

where in the north the summer makes a day,
of what is darkness . . . darkness that will come
to-morrow suddenly. Thank God at least
for this much of my life, that when you died
that when you kissed me dying, not a thought
of this made sorrow for you, that I too
was pure of even fear.

Oh yes, I thought,
still new in my insipid treadmill life,
(my father so late dead), and hopeful still
there might be something pleasant somewhere in it
some sudden fairy come, no doubt, to turn
my pumpkin to a chariot, I thought then
that I might plod, and plod, and drum the sounds
of useless facts into unwilling ears,
tease children with dull questions half the day,
then con dull answers in my room at night
ready for next day's questions, mend quill pens
and cut my fingers, add up sums done wrong
and never get them right; teach, teach, and teach –
what I half knew, or not at all – teach, teach
for years, a lifetime – I!

And yet, who knows?
it might have been, for I was patient once,
and willing, and meant well; it might have been
had I but still clung on in my first place –
a soft dull place, where mostly there were smiles
but never merry-makings; where all days
jogged on sedately busy, with no haste;
where all seemed measured out, but margins broad;
a dull home but a peaceful, where I felt
my pupils would be dear young sisters soon,
and felt their mother take me to her heart,
mother to all lonely harmless things.
But I must have a conscience, must blurt out
my great discovery of my ignorance!

And who required it of me? And who gained?
What did it matter for a more or less
the girls learnt in their schoolbooks, to forget
in their first season? We did well together:
they loved me and I them: but I went off
to housemaids' pay, six cross-grained brats to teach,
wrangles and jangles, doubts, disgrace . . . then this;
and they had a perfection found for them,
who has all ladies' learning in her head
abridged and scheduled, speaks five languages,
knows botany and conchology and globes,
draws, paints, plays, sings, embroiders, teaches all
on a patent method never known to fail:
and now they're finished and, I hear, poor things,
are the worst dancers and worst dressers out.
And where's the profit of those prison years
all gone to make them wise in lesson books?
Who wants his wife to know weeds' Latin names?
Who ever chose a girl for saying dates?
or asked if she had learnt to trace a map?

Well, well, the silly rules this silly world
makes about women! This is one of them.
Why must there be pretence of teaching them
what no-one ever cares that they should know,
what, grown out of the schoolroom, they cast off
like the schoolroom pinafore, no better fit
for any use of real grown-up life,
for any use of her who seeks and waits
the husband and the home, for any use,
for any shallowest pretence of use,
to her who has them? Do I not know this
I like my betters, that a woman's life,
her natural life, her good life, her one life,
is in her husband, God on earth to her,
and what she knows and what she can and is
is only good as it brings good to him?

Oh God, do I not know it? I the thing
of shame and rottenness, the animal
that feed men's lusts and prey on them, I, I,
who should not dare to take the name of wife
on my polluted lips, who in the word
hear but my own reviling, I know that.
I could have lived by that rule, how content:
my pleasure to make him some pleasure, pride
to be as he would have me, duty, care,
to fit all to his taste, rule my small sphere
to his intention; then to lean on him,
be guided, tutored, loved – no not that word,
that *loved* which between men and women means
all selfishness, all putrid talk, all lust,
all vanity, all idiocy – not loved
but cared for. I've been loved myself, I think,
some once or twice since my poor mother died,
but *cared for*, never: – that a word for homes,
kind homes, good homes, where simple children come
and ask their mother is this right or wrong,
because they know she's perfect, cannot err;
their father told them so, and he knows all,
being so wise and good and wonderful,
even enough to scorn her even at times
and tell her everything she does not know.
Ah the sweet nursery logic!

Fool! thrice fool!
do I hanker after that too? Fancy me
infallible nursery saint, live code of law!
me preaching! teaching innocence to be good! –
a mother!

Yet the baby thing that woke
and wailed an hour or two, and then was dead
was mine, and had he lived . . . why then my name
would have been mother . . .

From MEDEA IN ATHENS (23)

Oh smooth adder
who with fanged kisses changedst my natural blood
to venom in me, say, didst thou not find me
a grave and simple girl in a still home,
learning my spells for pleasant services
or to make sick beds easier? With me went
the sweet sound of friends' voices praising me:
all faces smiled on me, even lifeless things
seemed glad because of me; and I could smile
to every face, to everything, to trees,
to skies and waters, to the passing herds,
to the small thievish sparrows, to the grass
with sunshine through it, to the weeds bold flowers;
for all things glad and harmless seemed my kin,
and all seemed glad and harmless in the world.
Thou cam'st, and from the day thou, finding me
in Hecate's dim grove to cull my herbs,
didst burn my cheeks with kisses hot and strange,
the curse of thee compelled me. Lo I am
the wretch thou say'st; but wherefore? by whose work?
Who binding me with dreadful marriage oaths
in the midnight temple, led my treacherous flight
from home and father? Whose voice when I turned
desperate to save thee, on my own young brother,
my so loved brother, whose voice as I smote
nerved me, cried 'Brave Medea'? For whose ends
did I destroy the credulous girls, poor fools,
to slay their father? When have I been base,
when cruel, save for thee, until – Man, man,
wilt thou accuse my guilt? Whose is my guilt?
mine or thine, Jason? Oh, soul of my crimes,
how shall I pardon thee for what I am?

(24) XANTIPPE

As I stood
Ling'ring upon the threshold, half-concealed
By tender foliage, and my spirit light
With draughts of sunny weather, did I mark
An instant the gay group before mine eyes.
Deepest in shade, and facing where I stood,
Sat Plato, with his calm face and low brows
Which met above the narrow Grecian eyes,
The pale thin lips just parted to the smile,
Which dimpled that smooth olive of his cheek.
His head a little bent, sat Sokrates,
With one swart finger raised admonishing,
And on the air were borne his changing tones.
Low lounging at his feet, one fair arm thrown
Around his knee (the other, high in air
Brandished a brazen amphor, which yet rained
Bright drops of ruby on the golden locks
And temples with their fillets of the wine),
Lay Alkibiabes the beautiful.
And thus, with solemn tone, spake Sokrates:

'This fair Aspasia, which our Pericles
Hath brought from realms afar, and set on high
In our Athenian city, hath a mind,
I doubt not, of a strength beyond her race;
And makes employ of it, beyond the way
Of women nobly gifted: woman's frail –
Her body rarely stands the test of soul;
She grows intoxicate with knowledge; throws
The laws of custom, order, 'neath her feet,
Feasting at life's great banquet with wide throat.'

Then sudden, stepping from my leafy screen,
Holding the swelling wine-skin o'er my head,
With breast that heaved, and eyes and cheeks aflame,
Lit by a fury and a thought, I spake:

'By all great powers around us! can it be
That we poor women are empirical?
That gods who fashioned us did strive to make
Beings too fine, too subtly delicate,
With sense that thrilled response to ev'ry touch
of nature's, and their task is not complete?
That they have sent their half-completed work
To bleed and quiver here upon the earth?
To bleed and quiver, and to weep and weep,
To beat its soul against the marble walls
Of men's cold hearts, and then at last to sin!'

I ceased, the first hot passion stayed and stemmed
And frightened by the silence: I could see,
Framed by the arbour foliage, which the sun
In setting softly gilded with rich gold,
Those upturned faces, and those placid limbs:
Saw Plato's narrow eyes and niggard mouth,
Which half did smile and half did criticise,
One hand held up, the shapely fingers framed
To gesture of entreaty – 'Hush, I pray,
Do not disturb her; let us hear the rest;
Follow her mood, for here's another phase
Of your black-browed Xantippe . . .'
                                        Then I saw
Young Alkibiabes, with laughing lips
and half-shut eyes, contemptuous shrugging up
Soft snowy shoulders, till he brought the gold
Of flowing ringlets round about his breasts.
But Sokrates, all slow and solemnly,
Raised calm, his face to mine, and sudden spake:
'I thank thee for the wisdom which thy lips
Have thus let fall among us: prythee tell
From what high source, from what philosophies
Didst cull the sapient notion of thy words?'
Then stood I straight and silent for a breath,
Dumb, crushed with all that weight of cold contempt;

But swiftly in my bosom there uprose
A sudden flame, a merciful fury sent
To save me; with both angry hands I flung
The skin upon the marble, where it lay
Spouting red rills and fountains on the white;
The, all unheeding faces, voices, eyes,
I fled across the threshold, hair unbound –
White garment stained to redness – beating heart
Flooded with all the flowing tide of hopes
Which once had gushed out golden, now sent back
Swift to their sources, never more to rise; . . .

Mary Elizabeth Coleridge

A CLEVER WOMAN (25)

You thought I had the strength of men,
   Because with men I dared to speak,
And courted science now and then,
   And studied Latin for a week;
But woman's woman, even when
   She reads her Ethics in the Greek.

You thought me wiser than my kind;
   You thought me 'more than common tall';
You thought because I had a mind,
   That I could have no heart at all;
But woman's woman you will find,
   Whether she be great or small.

And then you needs must die – ah, well!
   I knew you not, you loved not me.
'Twas not because that darkness fell,
   You saw not what there was to see.
But I that saw and could not tell –
   O evil Angel, set me free!

THE WITCH (26)

I have walked a great while over the snow,
And I am not tall nor strong.
My clothes are wet, and my teeth are set,
And the way was hard and long.
I have wandered over the fruitful earth,
But I never came here before.
Oh, lift me over the threshold, and let me in
                    at the door!

The cutting wind is a cruel foe.
I dare not stand in the blast.
My hands are stone, and my voice a groan,

and the worst of death is past.
I am but a little maiden still,
My little white feet are sore.
Oh, lift me over the threshold, and let me in
at the door!

Her voice was the voice that women have,
Who plead for their heart's desire.
She came – she came – and the quivering flame
Sank and died in the fire.
It never was lit again on my hearth
Since I hurried across the floor,
To lift her over the threshold, and let her in
at the door!

(27) THE WHITE WOMEN*

Where dwell the lovely, wild white womenfolk,
Mortal to man?
They never bowed their necks beneath the yoke,
They dwelt alone when the first morning broke
And Time began.

Taller are they than man, and very fair,
Their cheeks are pale,
At sight of them the tiger in his lair,
The falcon hanging in the azure air,
The eagles quail.

The deadly shafts their nervous hands let fly
Are stronger than our strongest – in their form
Larger, more beauteous, carved amazingly,
And when they fight, the wild white women cry
The war-cry of the storm.

* From a legend of Malay, told by Hugh Clifford (note by M.E.C.).

Their words are not as ours. If man might go
   Among the waves of Ocean when they break
And hear them – hear the language of the snow
Falling on torrents – he might also know
   The tongue they speak.

Pure are they as the light; they never sinned,
   But when the rays of the eternal fire
Kindle the West, their tresses they unbind
And fling their girdles to the Western wind,
   Swept by desire.

Lo, maidens to the maidens then are born,
   Strong children of the maidens and the breeze,
Dreams are not – in the glory of the morn,
Seen through the gates of ivory and horn –
   More fair than these.

And none may find their dwelling. In the shade
   Primeval of the forest oaks they hide.
One of our race, lost in an awful glade,
Saw with his human eyes a wild white maid,
   And gazing, died.

Elizabeth Wolstenholme-Elmy

(28) *From* WOMAN FREE

XI

Marriage, which might have been a mateship sweet,
Where equal souls in hallowed converse meet,
Each aiding each the higher truths to find,
And raising body to the plane of mind, –
Man's baser will restrained to lower grade,
And woman's share a brainless bondage made;
Her only hope of thought or learning wide,
Some freer lot to seek than yoke forlorn of bride.

XII

Yet, as hetaira, – comrade, chamber-mate, –
(The ambiguous word bespoke her dubious state)
She, craving mental food, might but be guest
By paying with her body for the quest;
Conceding that, might lead a learned life, –
A licence vetoed to the legal wife, –
Might win great wealth, or build a lasting fame,
Not due to her the guilt that left the tinge of shame.

XIII

What guilt was there, apportion it aright
To him who fixed the gages of the fight;
Blame man, who, reckless of the woman's fate,
In greed for meaner pleasure lost the great;
Blame him, the vaunted sage, who knew her mind
Peer to his own in skill and wit refined,

Yet left the after ages to bemoan
The waste of woman* worth that dawned and died unknov

* * *

LVI

So he opes a vaster knowledge to the view,
Love points the way and woman holds the clue;
Nature on her the trustful office laid,
And arbiter of human fortune made;
With woman honoured, rises man to height,
With her degraded sinks again in night;
Yet still the wayward race has sluggish been
To learn the fealty due to Earth's advancing queen.

* Since these words were written, a letter from Mrs Mona Caird has been published by the 'Women's Emancipation Union', in which is said: 'So far from giving safety and balance to the "natural forces", these time-honoured restrictions, springing from a narrow theory which took its rise in a pre-scientific age, are fraught with the gravest dangers, creating a perpetual struggle and unrest, filling society with the perturbations and morbid developments of powers that ought to be spending themselves freely and healthfully on their natural objects. Anyone who has looked a little below the surface of women's lives can testify to the general unrest and nervous exhaustion or malaise among them, although each would probably refer her suffering to some cause peculiar to herself and her circumstances, never dreaming that she was the victim of an evil that gnaws at the very heart of society, making of almost every woman the heroine of a silent tragedy. I think few keen observers will deny that it is almost always the women of placid temperament, with very little sensibility, who are happy and contented; those of more highly wrought nervous systems and imaginative faculty, who are nevertheless capable of far greater joy than their calmer sisters, in nine cases out of ten are secretly intensely miserable. And the cause of this is not eternal and unalterable. The nervously organised being is *not* created to be miserable; but when intense vital energy is thwarted and misdirected – so long as the energy lasts – there must be intense suffering . . . It is only when resignation sets in, when the ruling order convinces at last and tires out the rebel nerves and the keen intelligence, that we know that the living forces are defeated, and that death has come to quiet the suffering. All this is waste of human force, and far worse than waste.'

[Author's note.]

LVII

For long, in jealousy for corporal power,
Had man contemned his sister's worthier dower;
What time his ruder feelings held the sway,
With little hope or hint of truer way;
Till on a wistful world has dawned benign
The prescience of a potency divine
Sleeping, unrecked of, deep in woman's heart
Waiting some kiss superne, into full life to start.

LVIII

Woman's own soul must seek and find that fay,
And wake it into light of quickening day;
Man's counsel helpful in that rack shall be
For all his learning rich return and fee;
His philosophic and chirurgic store,
To her imparted swell her innate store;
Till clothed with majesty of mind she stand,
Regent of Nature's will,* in heart, in head, in hand.

* 'Woman will grow into fitness for the sublime work which nature has given her to do, and man through her help and persuasion will spontaneously assume the relation of a co-operator in it. Finding that nature intends his highest good and and that of his species, through the emancipation and development of woman into the fulness of her powers, he will gratefully seek his own profit and happiness in harmonising himself with this method; he will honour it as nature's method, and woman as its chief executor; and will joyfully find that not only individuals, families, and communities, but nations, have been wisely dependent on her, in their more advanced conditions, for the good which can come only from the most perfect, artistic, and spiritual being who inhabits our earth' (Eliza W. Farnham, *Woman and Her Era*, Vol. II, p.423).

[Author's note.]

L.E. Morgan-Browne

THE PURPLE, WHITE AND GREEN (29)

(*Song of the Women's Social and Political Union*)
Tune: 'The Wearing of the Green'

Oh, Women dear, and did ye hear the news that's going round,
They think that prison bars will daunt those born on English ground;
They think they'll pile on penalties far harder than we've seen,
And gag the shouts of those who wear the purple, white and green.
But when we meet you women and you take us by the hand,
And you ask 'How are you doing?' we answer, 'doing grand!'
For it is the grandest movement that the world has ever seen,
And we're gathering in our thousands, wearing purple, white and green.

For it is the grandest movement the world has ever seen,
And we'll win the Vote for Women, wearing purple, white and green.

For forty years we talked and prayed, as gentle women do,
And oft the Cause has been betrayed by men we counted true;
But now the woman-worker roused, shouts with insistent note
For what she wants without delay – *and means to have* – the Vote!
So until the House of Commons heeds our knocking at the door,
And grants the freedom women claim, as men have claimed before;
Until the British woman votes like man for what she pays,
Until *that* day – so help us God! – our protests we will raise.

For it is the grandest movement the world has ever seen,
And we'll win the *Vote for Women* wearing purple, white and green.

Chorus

Hark to the fife! Hark to the drum!
W.S.P.U.
Who will obey the call and come?
W.S.P.U.
Purple a-flutter with White and Green,
W.S.P.U.

Purple stands for the loyal heart,
Loyal to cause and King
White for Purity, *Green* for hope
Bright hopes of Spring.

March and fight through the long, long night
That our children be brave and free!
March and fight for our one common right,
CITIZENS TO BE!

Christina Walsh

PRAYER TO ISIS (30)

('Slow and sustained')

O Isis, Mother of God, to thee I pray!
Forget not thy daughters here upon the earth.
Forgive them, for they have turned away from thee:
They who labour, suffer and weep
How much thou only knowest!
Have forgotten they are the daughters of Isis,
For they think they are the daughters & wives of men.
O come Isis and in thy majesty
Make thy throne in the hearts of women.
Teach them their right to honour,
And their queenship 'spite of suffering.
In the glorious motherhood stoop down
And raise their hearts to dwell with thee in proud and
  passionate joy.
O Isis, mother of God, hear my prayer.

A WOMAN TO HER LOVER (31)

('Proudly')

Do you come to me to bend me to your will
As conqueror to the vanquished
To make of me a bondslave
To bear you children, wearing out my life
In drudgery and silence
No servant will I be
If that be what you ask, O Lover (*'ironically'*) I refuse you!

(*'Mockingly-drawing room ballad style'*)

Or if you think to wed with one from heaven sent
Whose every deed and word and wish is golden
A wingless angel who can do no wrong
Go! – I am no doll to dress and sit for feeble worship
If that be what you ask, fool, I refuse you!

(*'Slowly'*)

Or if you think in me to find
A creature who will have no greater joy
Than gratify your clamorous desire,
My skin soft only for your fond caresses
My body supple only for your sense delight,
Oh shame, and pity and abasement.
Not for you the hand of any wakened woman of our time.

But Lover, if you ask of me
That I shall be your comrade, friend, and mate,
To live and work, to love and die with you,
That so together we may know the purity and height
Of passion, and of joy and sorrow,
Then O husband, I am yours forever
And our co-equal love will make the stars to laugh with joy
And we shall have the music of the spheres for bridal march
And to its circling fugue pass on, hand holding hand
Until we reach the very heart of God.

F.E.M. Macaulay

THE WOMEN'S MARSEILLAISE

(*Song of the Women's Social and Political Union*)

I

Arise ye daughters of a land
   That vaunts its liberty!
Make reckless rulers understand
   That women must be free,
   That women *will* be free.
Hark! Hark! The trumpet's calling!
   Who'd be a laggard in the fight?
   With victory even now in sight
And stubborn foemen backward falling.

Chorus:

To freedom's cause till death
   We swear our fealty.

Repeat:

March on! March on!
Face to the dawn,
   The dawn of liberty.

II

Arise! Thou pain or loss betide,
   Grudge naught of freedom's toll.
For what they loved the martyrs died;
   Are we of meaner soul?
   Are we of meaner soul?
Our comrades, greatly daring,
   Through prison bars have led the way:
   Who would not follow to the fray,
Their glorious struggle proudly sharing?

Cicely Hamilton

(33) THE MARCH OF THE WOMEN

(*Song of the Women's Social and Political Union*)

Shout, shout, up with your song!
Cry with the wind, for the dawn is breaking.
March, march, swing you along,
Wide blows our banner and hope is waking.
Song with its story, dreams with their glory,
Lo! they call and glad is their word.
Forward! hark how it swells,
Thunder of freedom, the voice of the Lord.

Long, long, we in the past,
Cowered in dread from the light of Heaven.
Strong, strong, stand we at last,
Fearless in faith and with sight new given.
Strength with its beauty, life with its duty,
(Hear the voice, oh, hear and obey),
These, these, beckon us on,
Open your eyes to the blaze of day!

Comrades, ye who have dared,
First in the battle to strive and sorrow.
Scorned, spurned, naught have you cared,
Raising your eyes to a wider morrow.
Ways that are weary, days that are dreary,
Toil and pain by faith ye have borne.
Hail, hail, victors ye stand,
Wearing the wreath that the brave have worn!

Life, strife, these two are one!
Naught can ye win but by faith and daring.
On, on, that ye have done,
But for the work of today preparing.
Firm in reliance, laugh a defiance,
(Laugh in hope, for sure is the end).
March, march, many as one,
Shoulder to shoulder and friend to friend.

Charlotte Mew

ON THE ROAD TO THE SEA (34)

We passed each other, turned and stopped for half an hour, then went our way,
I who make other women smile did not make you –
But no man can move mountains in a day.
So this hard thing is yet to do.

But first I want your life: – before I die I want to see
The world that lies behind the strangeness of your eyes,
There is nothing gay or green there for my gathering, it may be,
Yet on brown fields there lies
A haunting purple bloom: is there not something in grey skies
And in grey sea?
I want what world there is behind your eyes,
I want your life and you will not give it me.

Now, if I look, I see you walking down the years,
Young, and through August fields – a face, a thought, a swinging dream perched on a stile – ;
I would have liked (so vile we are!) to have taught you tears
But most to have made you smile.

To-day is not enough or yesterday: God sees it all –
Your length on sunny lawns, the wakeful rainy nights – ; tell me – ; (how vain to ask), but it is not a question – just a call – ;
Show me then, only your notched inches climbing up the garden wall,
I like you best when you are small.

Is this a stupid thing to say
Not having spent with you one day?
No matter; I shall never touch your hair
Or hear the little tick behind your breast,
Still it is there,
And as a flying bird
Brushes the branches where it may not rest
I have brushed your hand and heard
The child in you: I like that best

So small, so dark, so sweet; and were you also then too grave and wise?
Always I think. Then put your far off little hand in mine; – Oh! let it rest;
I will not stare into the early world beyond the opening eyes,
Or vex or scare what I love best.
But I want your life before mine bleeds away –
Here – not in heavenly hereafters – soon, –
I want your smile this very afternoon,
(The last of all my vices, pleasant people used to say,
I wanted and I sometimes got – the Moon!)

You know, at dusk, the last bird's cry,
And round the house the flap of the bat's low flight,
Trees that go black against the sky
And then – how soon the night!

No shadow of you on any bright road again,
And at the darkening end of this – what voice? whose kiss? As if you'd say!
It is not I who have walked with you, it will not be I who take away
Peace, peace, my little handful of the gleaner's grain
From your reaped fields at the shut of day.

Peace! Would you not rather die
Reeling, – with all the cannons at your ear?
So, at least, would I,
And I may not be here
To-night, to-morrow morning or next year.
Still I will let you keep your life a little while,
See dear?
I have made you smile.

(35) FAME

Sometimes in the over-heated house, but not for long,
Smirking and speaking rather loud,
I see myself among the crowd,
Where no one fits the singer to his song,
Or sifts the unpainted from the painted faces
Of the people who are always on my stair;
They were not with me when I walked in heavenly places;
But could I spare
In the blind Earth's great silences and spaces,
The din, the scuffle, the long stare
If I went back and it was not there?
Back to the old known things that are the new,
The folded glory of the gorse, the sweet-briar air,
To the larks that cannot praise us, knowing nothing of what we do
And the divine, wise trees that do not care
Yet, to leave Fame, still with such eyes and that bright hair!
God! If I might! And before I go hence
Take in her stead
To our tossed bed

One little dream, no matter how small, how wild.
Just now, I think I found it in a field, under a fence –
A frail, dead, new-born lamb, ghostly and pitiful and white,
    A blot upon the night,
The moon's dropped child!

THE TREES ARE DOWN (36)

– and he cried with a loud voice:
Hurt not the earth, neither the sea, nor the trees –
(Revelation.)

They are cutting down the great plane-trees at the end of the gardens.
For days there has been the grate of the saw, the swish of the branches as they fall,
The crash of the trunks, the rustle of trodden leaves,
With the 'Whoops' and the 'Whoas,' the loud common talk, the loud common laughs of the men, above it all.

I remember one evening of a long past Spring
Turning in at a gate, getting out of a cart, and finding a large dead rat in the mud of the drive.
I remember thinking: alive or dead, a rat was a god-forsaken thing,
But at least, in May, that even a rat should be alive.

The week's work here is as good as done. There is just one bough
  On the roped bole, in the fine grey rain,
      Green and high
      And lonely against the sky.
        (Down now! –)
      And but for that,
      If an old dead rat
Did once, for a moment, unmake the Spring, I might never have thought of him again.

It is not for a moment the Spring is unmade to-day;
These were great trees, it was in them from root to stem:
When the men with the 'Whoops' and the 'Whoas' have carted the whole of the whispering loveliness away
Half the Spring, for me, will have gone with them.

It is going now, and my heart has been struck with the hearts of the planes;
Half my life it has beat with these, in the sun, in the rains,
    In the March wind, the May breeze,
In the great gales that came over to them across the roofs from the great seas.
    There was only a quiet rain when they were dying;
    They must have heard the sparrows flying,
And the small creeping creatures in the earth where they were lying –
    But I, all day, I heard an angel crying:
        'Hurt not the trees.'

(37) THE QUIET HOUSE

When we were children old Nurse used to say
  The house was like an auction or a fair
  Until the lot of us were safe in bed.
  It has been quiet as the country-side
  Since Ted and Janey and then Mother died
And Tom crossed Father and was sent away.
After the lawsuit he could not hold up his head,
  Poor Father, and he does not care
  For people here, or to go anywhere.

To get away to Aunt's for that week-end
  Was hard enough; (since then, a year ago,
  He scarcely lets me slip out of his sight –)
At first I did not like my cousin's friend,
  I did not think I should remember him:
  His voice has gone, his face is growing dim
And if I like him now I do not know.
  He frightened me before he smiled –
  He did not ask me if he might –
  He said that he would come one Sunday night,
  He spoke to me as if I were a child.

No year has been like this that has just gone by;
  It may be that what Father says is true,
If things are so it does not matter why:
  But everything has burned, and not quite through.
  The colours of the world have turned
  To flame, the blue, the gold has burned
In what used to be such a leaden sky.
When you are burned quite through you die.

Red is the strangest pain to bear;
In Spring the leaves on the budding trees;
In Summer the roses are worse than these,
More terrible than they are sweet:
A rose can stab you across the street
Deeper than any knife:
And the crimson haunts you everywhere –
Thin shafts of sunlight, like the ghosts of reddened swords have struck our stair
As if, coming down, you had split your life.

I think that my soul is red
Like the soul of a sword or a scarlet flower:
But when these are dead
They have had their hour.

I shall have had mine, too,
For from head to feet,
I am burned and stabbed half through,
And the pain is deadly sweet.

The things that kill us seem
Blind to the death they give:
It is only in our dream
The things that kill us live.

The room is shut where Mother died,
The other rooms are as they were,
The world goes on the same outside,
The sparrows fly across the Square,
The children play as we four did there,
The trees grow green and brown and bare,
The sun shines on the dead Church spire,
And nothing lives here but the fire,
While Father watches from his chair
Day follows day
The same, or now and then, a different grey,
Till, like his hair,
Which Mother said was wavy once and bright,
They will all turn white.

To-night I heard a bell again –
Outside it was the same mist of fine rain,
The lamps just lighted down the long, dim street,
No one for me –
I think it is myself I go to meet:
I do not care; some day I *shall* not think; I shall not *be*!

Alice Meynell

(38) SUMMER IN ENGLAND, 1914

On London fell a clearer light;
    Caressing pencils of the sun
Defined the distances, the white
    Houses transfigured one by one,
The 'long, unlovely street' impearled.
O what a sky has walked the world!

Most happy year! And out of town
    The hay was prosperous, and the wheat;
The silken harvest climbed the down:
    Moon after moon was heavenly-sweet.
Stroking the bread within the sheaves,
Looking 'twixt apples and their leaves.

And while this rose made round her cup,
    The armies died convulsed. And when
This chaste young silver sun went up
    Softly, a thousand shattered men,
One wet corruption, heaped the plain,
After a league-long throb of pain.

Flower following tender flower; and birds,
    And berries, and benignant skies
Made thrive the serried flocks and herds. –
    Yonder are men shot through the eyes;
        Love, hide thy face
From man's unpardonable race.

Who said, 'No man hath greater love than this,
    To die to serve his friend'?
So these have loved us all unto the end.
    Chide thou no more, O thou unsacrificed!
The soldier dying dies upon a kiss,
    The very kiss of Christ.

IN SLEEP (39)

I dreamt (no 'dream' awake – a dream indeed)
A wrathful man was talking in the park:
'Where are the Higher Powers, who know our need
And leave us in the dark?

'There are no Higher Powers; there is no heart
In God no love' – his oratory here,
Taking the paupers' and the cripples' part,
Was broken by a tear.

And then it seemed that One who did create
Compassion, who alone invented pity,
Walked, as though called, in at that north-east gate,
Out from the muttering city;

Threaded the little crowd, trod the brown grass.
Bent o'er the speaker close, saw the tear rise,
And saw Himself, as one looks in a glass,
In those impassioned eyes.

EASTER NIGHT (40)

All night had shout of men and cry
Of woeful women filled his way;
Until that noon of sombre sky
On Friday, clamour and display
Smote Him; no solitude had He,
No silence, since Gethsemane.

Public was Death; but Power, but Might,
But Life again, but Victory,
Were hushed within the dead of night,
The shutter'd dark, the secrecy.
And all alone, alone, alone,
He rose again behind the stone.

(41) A FATHER OF WOMEN

AD SOROREM E.B.

'Thy father was transfused into thy blood.'
(Dryden, *Ode to Mrs Anne Killigrew*)

Our father works in us,
The daughters of his manhood. Not undone
Is he, not wasted, though transmuted thus,
And though he left no son.

Therefore on him I cry
To arm me: 'For my delicate mind a casque,
A breastplate for my heart, courage to die,
Of thee, captain, I ask.

'Nor strengthen only; press
A finger on this violent blood and pale,
Over this rash will let thy tenderness
A while pause, and prevail.

'And shepherd-father, thou
Whose staff folded my thoughts before my birth,
Control them now I am of earth, and now
Thou art no more of earth.

'O liberal, constant, dear,
Crush in my nature the ungenerous art
Of the inferior; set me high, and here,
Here garner up thy heart!'

Like to him now are they,
The million living fathers of the War –
Mourning the crippled world, the bitter day –
Whose striplings are no more.

The crippled world! Come then,
Fathers of women with your honour in trust,
Approve, accept, know them daughters of men,
Now that your sons are dust.

The Meeting

ON READING CONTEMPORARY POETRY 1920–80

Introduction

Milton and Chaucer, Herbert, Herrick, Gray,
Rupert, and you forgotten others, say –
Are there slow rivers and bridges where you have
gone away?
What has your spirit found?
What wider lot?
Some days in spring do you come back at will,
And tread with weightless feet the ancient ground?

Frances Cornford (42)

I rode with my darling in the dark wood at night
And suddenly there was an angel burning bright
Come with me or go far away he said
But do not stay alone in the dark wood at night.

Stevie Smith (48)

and now in streets where only white
mac or car metal catches the falling
light, if we sing of
the red and the blue and the texture of goat hair,
there is no deceit in our prophecy:
for even now our brackish waters can
be sweetened by a strange tree.

Elaine Feinstein (60)

Mole he sleeps deep, his velvet nurtured by
The proper dryness, cohesion, in the earth
His only place, he knows,
Safe from the pull of the malign dews of the stars
The vast cold glitter, thin twanging in the spheres
That draws men, crazy, across shadeless tundra.

Jenny Joseph (66)

The purpose of the selection of poems that now follows is to support you in reading contemporary poetry by women. When we consider poetry written a century or so ago, patterns emerge. Exploration of work much closer to us in time and experience is likely to be more tentative. We are less sure of where we're going; we are less sure of the worth of what we're doing; and our experience is less likely to have been charted.

The experience of tentatively creating a context in which to experience contemporary literature is shared equally by those presenting books on contemporary literature and the reader wondering how and what to read.

From this point in this collection onwards, a decision has been taken to throw the emphasis firmly on literature that is being created now – both poetry that can be identified with a mainstream poetical tradition and feminist poetry more polemical in tone. Some poetry that may be defined as 'feminist' is to be found in the final section of the collection.

In choosing to focus on contemporary poetry in this way, the possibility of a historical presentation of all those who seemed to be important poets ten, twenty, thirty or more years ago has been sacrificed. In a sense, though, the presence of such writers is implied in the works presented here. For example, Anne Stevenson's 'Correspondence' consciously draws on the work of writers writing at the time of major events in the family whose history she is tracing. In the anguished 'From an Asylum' (52) the voices of Anne Sexton and Sylvia Plath are very evident; it is not plagiarism, though there may be an element of serious parody. Poetry of worth doesn't come from nowhere: previous generations of writers have made it possible for the present generation to write as they do. There are writers today using some of the traditional language of poetry and the traditional subject matter and there always have been. But from time to time poets make innovations. Chaucer, at the end of the fourteenth century, was the first to create poetry in English that is recognisable to us. Somebody had to write the first work of modern Greek literature after the liberation from Turkish rule – and he had to teach himself Greek to do it; but the job of the serious poet has always been to commemorate moral and artistic truth so the next generation may have something to learn from, and to hand on. So behind the writers included here are many others, and when you have read the ones in this book, your next step may be to find out who those others are.

In 'The Meeting' by Nicki Jackowska (81), a man opens a car door. A woman walks towards the car. The report of the incident is repeated five times each with a different accumulation of strange, dreamlike, descriptive detail. The mystery of the encounter is not directly explained. There is the sense of ideas and associations accumulating around a dream.

Many of the poems in this section have as their central core of meaning the encounter with the unfamiliar, that which is outside ordinary, everyday experience. In these poems we encounter angels, magic trees, timeless music, spirit-haunted rivers, the sea, the moon, the unborn child, strange formless monsters, goddesses and spirits. The stuff of fairy-tales maybe – but more profoundly the encounter, the Meeting, is with the Muse; for magic rivers, songs, trees, landscapes and spirits have always been part of the traditional symbolic language of poetry which has as its purpose no mere reporting, but the re-creation of inspiration.

The Poets

FRANCES CORNFORD 1886–1960 (42) (43) (44) (45) (46). Frances Cornford was born in Cambridge, the daughter of Sir Francis Darwin (Reader in Botany, author and fifth child of Charles Darwin and Ellen Crofts). She was educated at home. Apart from her half-brother Bernard Darwin, the son of Francis by an earlier marriage, she was an only child. Many details of her early life are recorded in *Period Piece* by Gwen Raverat. She married Francis Macdonald Cornford (Fellow of Trinity College, Cambridge, and subsequently Professor of Ancient Philosophy, Cambridge, authority on Plato and Aristotle), in 1909; and lived at Conduit Head, Madingley Road (one mile outside Cambridge) most of her life, with occasional excursions to Europe and one to America. They had five children – Helena Darwin, Rupert John, Christopher Francis, Hugh Wordsworth, Ruth Clare – and all at present survive except John Cornford, poet and Communist activist, who was killed on his twenty-first birthday fighting for the Spanish republic in December 1936 (see J. Galassi, *Understand the Weapon, Understand the Wound*, 1976). Frances Cornford died in Cambridge. Her manuscripts, letters and notebooks are now in the British Museum. She published nine collections of which the most recent were *Travelling Home, Collected Poems* and *On a Calm Shore* (1948, 1954 and 1960). (Biographical information supplied by Christopher Cornford.)

STEVIE SMITH 1902–71 (47) (48) (49) (50) (51). Stevie Smith was born in Hull, Yorkshire, on 20 September 1902. She was educated at Palmers Green High School, London, and the North London Collegiate School for Girls. She worked as secretary to Neville Pearson of Newnes Publishing Company London from 1923 to 1953. She wrote and broadcast from time to time for the BBC. She received the Cholmondeley Award in 1966 and the Queen's Gold Medal for Poetry in 1969. She died on 8 March 1971. See *Collected Poems* (1978), *Me Again* (1982), *Novel on Yellow Paper* (first published in 1936), *Over the Frontier* (1938) and *The Holiday* (1949).

ANNE STEVENSON (52). Anne Stevenson was born in England of American parents in 1933. She was educated in Ann Arbor, Michigan, where she graduated from the University of Michigan in 1954. She was at that time planning to be a cellist, but married and came to England instead, where she taught and worked for a publisher in London until she was divorced and returned to Michigan for an M.A. Her first book of poems, *Living in America*, appeared in 1965, followed by *Reversals* in 1969 and, in the 1970s, *Travelling Behind Glass, Correspondences* and *Enough of Green.* A new book of poems, *Minute by Glass Minute*, appeared in the autumn of 1982. Anne Stevenson has lived in New England and in the South and Midwest of America, in Scotland and in Wales where she was co-founder of the Poetry Bookshop with Michael Farley; in 1981 she was appointed Northern Arts Literary Fellow at the Universities of Newcastle and Durham.

ANNA ADAMS (53) (54). Anna Adams was born in Richmond, Surrey, in 1926. She was educated at Harrow Art School and Hornsey College of Art, going through from the junior department to an N.D.D. in Painting and Sculpture. She taught art to children, worked as a designer and made terracottas in the 1950s. Her first published essays appeared in *Freedom* in 1951, followed by an essay in *Nursery World* about babies. She wrote articles in the *Guardian* in the 1960s but 'after a dangerous illness in 1960 I really put my back into poetry – my preferred field – trying to master the craft as an instrument for truth mining . . . I consider that I write for my life rather than my living.' Her first poems were published in 1969, followed by four more pamphlets as well as *Rainbow Plantation Outposts, Memorial Tree Parabola* and *Unchanging Seas* before *A Reply to Intercepted Mail* was published in 1979. Her poems have been included in P.E.N. and Arts Council and other anthologies and have appeared in *Poetry Review, Pennine Platform, Outposts, Stand, Encounter, P.N. Review, Scottish Field* and broadcast on Radio 3 'Poetry Now', Radio 4 Schools Programmes and BBC Television 'Closedown' programmes.

ELAINE FEINSTEIN (55) (56) (57) (58) (59) (60) (77). Elaine Feinstein was born in Bootle, Lancashire, in 1930 and brought up in the Midlands, in Leicester. She is of Russian Jewish descent. She read English at Newnham College, Cambridge, took part 1 Bar finals in law in London, worked briefly for Cambridge University Press and taught in various institutions. She married Dr Arnold Feinstein, a biochemist, in 1956. They have three sons. 'I began writing as a poet, with the particular excitement in language that only poetry can satisfy, and only turned to writing novels in 1969. All the same, I have written seven novels. I regard translations as very much continuous with my own work as a poet, and have only translated poets whose work, in some way, relates to my own. I identify very strongly with Tsvetayeva, as a woman because she combined the stamina to support a family in great hardship for more than twenty years while going on writing through everything, though of course I say that humbly, since she is among the greatest poets of the century.' (Two extracts from Elaine Feinstein's translation of Tsvetayeva's 'Poem of the End' are included in this collection (77).) Recent publications include *The Survivors* (1982), *The Silent Areas: Short Stories* (1980), *Some Unease and Angels: Selected Poems* (1977) and *The Ecstasy of Dr Miriam Garner* (1976).

RUTH FAINLIGHT (61) (62). Ruth Fainlight was born in New York City. She was educated at schools in America and England and is married to Alan Sillitoe, the novelist and poet. She has a considerable reputation as a poet and short-story writer. In addition, she translates from Spanish, Portuguese and Catalan. Her poetry collections include *The Region's Violence* (1973), *Another Full Moon* (1975), *To See the Matter Clearly* (1977), *Sibyls and Others* (1980).

JENNY JOSEPH (63) (64) (65) (66). 'The only details I care to set down are in connection with books published or forthcoming and other work. I have published three poetry collections: *The Unlooked For Season* (1960), *Rose in the Afternoon* (1974), *The Thinking Heart* (1979). A fourth collection, *Beyond Descartes,* is forthcoming. My unpublished work in prose and verse, *Persephone,* was completed in 1979. All this seems much more relevant to the anthology than where I live and how many children I've got.'

FRANCES HOROVITZ (67) (68) (69). Frances Horovitz was born in London in 1938. She was educated at Bristol University and at the Royal Academy of Dramatic Art. She is well known as a poetry reader for the BBC and the Open University. She gives many live readings of her own and others' poetry. Her current poetry performances include 'Thomas Hardy and His Women' and 'Light and Shade: The Poetry of John Keats', both with Robert Gittings, also the poetry of Sappho with Paul Roche. She is a tutor for the Arvon Foundation. She was formerly married to the poet Michael Horovitz, by whom she has one son, Adam. She now lives with the poet and critic Roger Garfitt. Publications include *The High Tower, Water over Stone, Wall* (with three other poets) and, in 1982, *Rowlerstone Haiku* with Roger Garfitt.

PENELOPE SHUTTLE (70) (71) (72) (73) (74). Penelope Shuttle was born in Middlesex in 1947 and now lives in Cornwall. She is married to Peter Redgrove, and has a young daughter. She began her writing career in her early teens, publishing poetry in numerous magazines. She has produced five novels and two radio plays. A main concern in all these works is the continuation of the vigorous and versatile capabilities of poetry into the areas of prose and drama – an imaginative mingling of modes to create an individual and living style. Her most recent publication is her first major collection of poems, *The Orchard Upstairs* (1981). Penelope Shuttle has collaborated with Peter Redgrove on two novels and a book of verse but their major work together has been the pioneer study, *The Wise Wound,* a psychological study of the menstrual cycle, a book which has contributed greatly to new perceptions of identity in women.

VIVIENNE FINCH (75) (76). Vivienne Finch is a freelance journalist and translator. Her articles have appeared in magazines as varied as *Cosmopolitan* and *She* through to *Child Education* and *Special Education* and she has given readings throughout the U.K. in colleges, bookshops and galleries, as well as festivals. She belonged to a poetry theatre group, ran a poetry workshop for several years and co-edited Tangent Books, producing over several years a body of experimental chapbooks and magazines of poetry and prose. Currently she is working as a researcher for the BBC, having broadcast regularly. Several books of her poetry have been published, including *Green Stares Back, The Only Generic, The Possible Dark* and *The Owl Master.* The latter has had a varied and successful 'life', having been adapted for children's television, produced as a play in a fringe theatre production, and performed by the Canadian Broadcasting Corporation in a stereophonic workshop programme. A book of her translations of Pierre Reverdy has also been published. Her poetry has appeared in many magazines in Britain as well as in the United States, Canada, France and Australia (translated into French by Claude Minière). 'My book *Interactions* is to be read as an overlapping sequence of dialogues with other texts, other writers. Its integrated remarks and silences remind us that "knowledge" of women in any one age is constantly open to rupture and revision. We read the road or sky ahead as any book, and what we perceive, as such, is language – a creation of our own need, part of the great diversion. Fear, hope-loss, gain – these are the ongoing actions of the dream of ego; the self-perpetuating, self-maintaining structure is self-deception. "Twenty million young women rose to their feet with the cry – we shall not be dictated to – and promptly became stenographers," wrote Chesterton of female independence in the twentieth century. But since desire always goes towards that which is our direct opposite, it forces us to love that which will make us suffer.'

MARINA TSVETAYEVA 1892–1941 (translated by Elaine Feinstein) (77). Marina Tsvetayeva was born in Moscow in 1892. Her father was a professor of art history and her mother was a pianist. Her first book of poems was written when she was only eighteen, published in 1910 and very favourably reviewed by leading critics. Although she opposed the Revolution, and her husband (Sergei Efron) fought on the White side, she did not leave Russia until 1922, after the Moscow famine in which one of her children died. She then lived in Prague, in which some of her greatest poetry is set, and afterwards in Berlin and Paris, where she was initially welcomed enthusiastically by the Russian emigrés. However, as she continued to be involved with poets who remained in Russia, she gradually became more isolated. Her husband returned to Russia, having become a Soviet sympathiser, and she followed him back there in 1939. He was shot, however, most probably on entering the country. At the outbreak of war with Germany, she was evacuated to Yelabuga, and there, alone and unable to find work, she hanged herself in 1941.

NICKI JACKOWSKA (78) (79) (80) (81). Nicki Jackowska was born in Brighton, Sussex, in 1942. She began writing at the age of seventeen. From 1963 to 1965 she trained as an actress and spent three years in the professional theatre. She moved to Cornwall in 1968 where she founded and published *Poetry St Ives*, funded by Southwest Arts, and worked with other writers on poetry/music workshops and performances. From 1969 to 1972 she worked with her own performing company, Tower of Babel, on plays and shows written by the group. From 1969 to 1970 she was the South-west coordinator to the Arts Councils New Activities Committee, directing an arts festival of new work in St Ives in 1970. From 1974 to 1978 she took an honours degree and an M.A. in philosophy at Sussex University. She now works as a poet and novelist on performances and readings of her own work and also as an actress. She also tutors creative writing courses for the Arvon Foundation, Centre for Continuing Education at Sussex University, Writers in Schools, for community arts, etc. In 1982 she received a C.D. Lewis writing fellowship. Recent books include *The House that Manda Built* (1981), *Incubus* (1981), *Doctor Marbles and Marianne: A Romance* (1982), *Earthwalks* (1982). 'The basic energy of my work concentrates around a number of questions. The poems themselves pose questions, and give only half answers. We are still dominated by the need for absolute clarity. How can poems be that? They extend inwards as well as down the page. For the answers can only come from the responding human being who completes or extends the picture or structure of meaning that is being transmitted. I don't write about a purely female experience. I write about a dimension of experience that men find it more difficult than women to explore, a dimension that is part of being fully human for either sex. I'd expect the same to be true of novels and poems written by men. The areas of exploration for me are human, not female specially. I count it as an enrichment to be in touch with such things, even if painful.'

FRANKIE ARMSTRONG (82) (83) (84) (85). Born in Cumberland, Frankie began singing when the first folk boom hit Britain in 1957. Since 1962 she has built up a repertoire of British traditional songs and ballads, which, along with the contemporary British songs, still form the bulk of her musical vocabulary. Frankie owes much of the early development of her singing style to the influence of A.L. Lloyd and the traditional women singers of the U.K. and Ireland. In addition to her work within the folk clubs she has performed at many folk and arts festivals, including Edinburgh, Aldeburgh and York community arts centres; theatres; for anti-nuclear and women's organisations. She has toured in the U.S., Canada, Holland, France, Germany, Denmark and Sweden. Her repertoire includes rural, industrial, music hall and contemporary songs; those of her own and of song writers such as Leon Rosselson and Bertolt Brecht. She selects and interprets songs that explore and express personal and social relationships, especially those that focus on the experiences of women. She was involved in compiling a collection of 100 songs about women's lives – *My Song Is My Own* with Kathy Henderson and Sandra Kerr and the record of the same name which also includes Alison McMorland. Her solo records are *Lovely on the Water, Songs and Ballads, Out of Love, Hope and Suffering* and *The Music Plays So Grand.* Recently she has been leading an increasing number of vocal workshops designed to help singers and non-singers alike to liberate their voices. These workshops give the opportunity to call on the skills of her other career as a social and group worker, which she has also pursued for the past eighteen years.

Frances Cornford

IN THE BACKS (42)

Too many of the dead, some I knew well,
Have smelt this unforgotten river smell,
Liquid and old and dank,
And on the tree-dark, lacquered, slowly passing stream
Have seen the boats come softly as in dream
Past the green bank.
So Camus, reverend sire, came footing slow
Three hundred years ago,
And Milton paced the avenue of trees
In miracle of sun and shade as now,
The fresh-attempted glorious cadences
Behind his youthful brow.

Milton and Chaucer, Herbert, Herrick, Gray,
Rupert, and you forgotten others, say –
Are there slow rivers and bridges where you have gone
  away?
What has your spirit found?
What wider lot?
Some days in spring do you come back at will,
And tread with weightless feet the ancient ground?
O say, if not,
Why is this air so sacred and so still?

SUMMER BEACH (43)

For how long known this boundless wash of light,
  This smell of purity, this gleaming waste,
This wind? This brown, strewn wrack how old a sight,
  These pebbles round to touch and salt to taste.

See, the slow marbled heave, the liquid arch,
  Before the waves' procession to the land
Flowers in foam; the ripples onward march,
  Their last caresses on the pure hard sand.

For how long known these bleaching corks, new-made
   Smooth and enchanted from the lapping sea?
Since first I laboured with a wooden spade
   Against this background of Eternity.

(44) FOR M.S.
SINGING *FRUHLINGSGLAUBE* IN 1945

'Nun muss sich alles, alles wenden'

Here are the Schubert *Lieder.* Now begin.

First the accompaniment,
Heart-known and heaven sent
And so divinely right
The inmost spirit laughs with sure delight.

And now the fountain of the melody.

To your forgiven fields I am entered in,
Spring of my adolescence, Spring of the world,
Where every secret lime-leaf is unfurled.
Where all's made well again, yet more's to be –

Then why this misery?

Because, O enemy alien heart, we fear
That you are lost on your demoniac shore,
And we deny that in your music – here
Is your unchanged, unchanging innocent core.

(45) THE SCHOLAR

You often went to breathe a timeless air
And walk with those you loved, perhaps the most.
You spoke to Plato. You were native there.
Like one who made blind Homer sing to him,

You visited the caves where sirens swim
Their deep indented coast.
With us you seemed
A quiet happy sailor come of late
From those strange seas you best could navigate,
Knowing a world that others only dreamed.
Almost we looked for spray upon your hair,
Who met you, silent footed on the stair,
Like an Elysian ghost.
So on that day
You left us on a deep withdrawing tide,
We dared not beg you, with one sigh, to stay
Or turn from your discoveries aside.

INSCRIPTION FOR A WAYSIDE SPRING (46)

ALL MEN FROM ALL LANDS
KNEEL BEFORE YOU GO
CUP YOUR HANDS
LIKE A BOWL
LET ME OVERFLOW
READ WHAT THESE WORDS TELL
LEAN DOWN AND KNOW
EACH ONE
BESIDE MY BRINK
BEND DOWN LOW
LOST SON
SAD DAUGHTER
BEND DOWN AND DRINK
I AM THE WATER OF THE WELL
THAT MAKES MEN WHOLE
I AM THE COLD WATER
THAT RESTORES YOUR SOUL

(47) THE RIVER GOD

I may be smelly and I may be old,
Rough in my pebbles, reedy in my pools,
But where my fish float by I bless their swimming
And I like the people to bathe in me, especially women.
But I can drown the fools
Who bathe too close to the weir, contrary to rules.
And they take a long time drowning
As I throw them up now and then in a spirit of clowning.
Hi yih, yippity-yap, merrily I flow,
O I may be an old foul river but I have plenty of go.
Once there was a lady who was too bold
She bathed in me by the tall black cliff where the water
runs cold,
So I brought her down here
To be my beautiful dear.
Oh will she stay with me will she stay
This beautiful lady, or will she go away?
She lies in my beautiful deep river bed with many a weed
To hold her, and many a waving reed.
Oh who would guess what a beautiful white face lies there
Waiting for me to smooth and wash away the fear
She looks at me with. Hi Yih, do not let her
Go. There is no one on earth who does not forget her
Now. They say I am a foolish old smelly river
But they do not know of my wide original bed
Where the lady waits, with her golden sleepy head.
If she wishes to go I will not forgive her.

(48) I RODE WITH MY DARLING...

I rode with my darling in the dark wood at night
And suddenly there was an angel burning bright
Come with me or go far away he said
But do not stay alone in the dark wood at night.

My darling grew pale he was responsible
He said we should go back it was reasonable
But I wished to stay with the angel in the dark wood
at night.

My darling said goodbye and rode off angrily
And suddenly I rode after him and came to a cornfield
Where had my darling gone and where was the angel now?
The wind bent the corn and drew it along the ground
And the corn said, Do not go alone in the dark wood.

Then the wind drew more strongly and the black clouds
covered the moon
And I rode into the dark wood at night.

There was a light burning in the trees but it was not
the angel
And in the pale light stood a tall tower without windows
And a mean rain fell and the voice of the tower spoke,
Do not stay alone in the dark wood at night.

The walls of the pale tower were heavy, in a heavy mood
The great stones stood as if resisting without belief.
Oh how sad sighed the wind, how disconsolately,
Do not ride alone in the dark wood at night.

Loved I once my darling? I love him not now.
Had I a mother beloved? She lies far away.
A sister, a loving heart? My aunt a noble lady?
All all is silent in the dark wood at night.

MY HAT (49)

Mother said if I wore this hat
I should be certain to get off with the right sort of chap
Well look where I am now, on a desert island
With so far as I can see no one at all on hand
I know what has happened though I suppose Mother

wouldn't see
This hat being so strong has completely run away with me
I had the feeling it was beginning to happen the moment I
put it on
What a moment that was as I rose up, I rose up like a flying
swan
As strong as a swan too, why see how far my hat has flown me
away
It took us a night to come and then a night and a day
And all the time the swan wing in my hat waved beautifully
Ah, I thought, How this hat becomes me.
First the sea was dark but then it was pale blue
And still the wing beat and we flew and we flew
A night and a day and a night, and by the old right way
Between the sun and the moon we flew until morning day.
It is always early morning here on this peculiar island
The green grass grows into the sea on the dipping land
Am I glad I am here? Yes, well, I am,
It's nice to be rid of Father, Mother and the young man
There's just one thing causes me a twinge of pain,
If I take my hat off, shall I find myself home again?
So in this early morning land I always wear my hat
Go home, you see, well I wouldn't run a risk like that.

(50) CHILDE ROLANDINE

Dark was the day for Childe Rolandine the artist
When she went to work as a secretary-typist
And as she worked she sang this song
Against oppression and the rule of wrong:

It is the privilege of the rich
To waste the time of the poor
To water with tears in secret
A tree that grows in secret
That bears fruit in secret

That ripened falls to the ground in secret
And manures the parent tree
Oh the wicked tree of hatred and the secret
The sap rising and the tears falling.

Likely also, sang the Childe, my soul will fry in hell
Because of this hatred, while in heaven my employer does
well
And why should he not, exacerbating though he be but
generous
Is it his fault I must work at a work that is tedious?
Oh heaven sweet heaven keep my thoughts in their night
den
Do not let them by day be spoken.

But then she sang, Ah why not? tell all, speak, speak,
Silence is vanity, speak for the whole truth's sake.

And rising she took the bugle and put it to her lips, crying:
There is a Spirit feeds on our tears, I give him mine,
Mighty human feelings are his food
Passion and grief and joy his flesh and blood
That he may live and grow fat we daily die
This cropping One is our immortality.

Childe Rolandine bowed her head and in the evening
Drew the picture of the spirit from heaven.

THE GALLOPING CAT (51)

Oh I am a cat that likes to
Gallop about doing good
So
One day when I was
Galloping about doing good, I saw
A Figure in the path; I said:
Get off! (Be-
cause

I am a cat that likes to
Gallop about doing good)
But he did not move, instead
He raised his hand as if
To land me a cuff
So I made to dodge so as to
Prevent him bringing it orf,
Un-for-tune-ately I slid
On a banana skin
Some Ass had left instead
Of putting in the bin. So
His hand caught me on the cheek
I tried
To lay his arm open from wrist to elbow
With my sharp teeth
Because I am
A cat that likes to gallop about doing good.
Would you believe it?
He wasn't there
My teeth met nothing but air,
But a Voice said: Poor cat,
(Meaning me) and a soft stroke
Came on me head
Since when
I have been bald.
I regard myself as
A martyr to doing good.
Also I heard a swoosh
As of wings, and saw
A halo shining at the height of
Mrs. Gubbins's backyard fence,
So I thought: What's the good
of galloping about doing good
When angels stand in the path
And do not do as they should
Such as having an arm to be bitten off
All the same I

Intend to go on being
A cat that likes to
Gallop about doing good
So
Now with my bald head I go
Chopping the untidy flowers down, to
and fro,
An' scooping up the grass to show
Underneath
The cinder path of wrath
Ha ha ha ha, ho,
Angels aren't the only ones who do
not know
What's what and that
Galloping about doing good
Is a full-time job
That needs
An experienced eye of earthly
Sharpness, worth I dare say
(If you'll forgive a personal note)
A good deal more
Than all that skyey stuff
Of angels that make so bold as
To pity a cat like me that
Gallops about doing good.

Anne Stevenson

(52) FROM AN ASYLUM:
KATHY CHATTLE TO HER MOTHER, RUTH ARBEITER

The Good Samaritan Hospital, New York, 2 May 1954

Mother,

If I am *where* I am
because I am *what* I am
will you forgive me?

God knows I have fought you long enough . . .
soft puppet on the knuckles of your conscience, or
dangling puritanical doll made of duty and habit
and terror and self-revulsion.
At what cost
keeping balance on invisible threads?
At what price
dancing in a sweater set and pearls
on the stage sets of your expectations?

Yes she was a nice girl!
Yes she was good!
Got married. Had a baby.
Just as she should.

Her head was made of walnut
His body of wood.
Then they had a little baby
made of flesh and blood.

Oh mother, poor mother!
Daddy thinks I'm wicked.
Here they think I'm crazy.
Please think I'm dead.

Dead, yes, and watching
from that safe, safe distance.
There. Your stubborn shoulders.
Tight smile.
Head in relief, tilted a little,

tense with controlling intelligence.
How can I make you believe
I am myself – a self –
only when dying alive?
Without some interior self-murder
I am blank, void.
The face which I know must be watching
but is never there.
To the flow, you might say, of my experience
what a screen is to the flow of a film.

When I had little Libby, yes,
I was almost real.
But used. Used up.
Almost killed, being able to feel.
'Motherhood will settle her nerves,'
Daddy said, who was never a mother.
I knew in the coil of my head
how I hated her! Hated her!

Christ, how she howled!
And nothing I could feed her . . .
my milk, canned milk, powdered milk, goat's milk . . .
nothing would soothe her.
The doctor? Sympathetic but busy
And I, pouring breastmilk and blood . . .
uncontainable tears . . .
Once, in a quiet hour, I wrote to you.
Frank burned the letter.

He had begun to be gnawed.
Fine unseen teeth were
gnawing him . . . whittling him.
Wife
forcing him into the prison of a family.
Baby
shaping him into the
middle-class, money-earning

ulcered American Dad
Frank's maleness, idealism . . .
self-flattering, easy conceit
never could admit.

Remember when he bought us that
crazy red, ramshackle farmhouse?
Miles out in the used-to-be country?
Well, his sports car, his sideburns,
his Scotch tweeds and 2 a.m. barbecues
gave our wife-swapping, beef-eating neighbors
some unthreatening entertainments!

But by that time we were enemies.
By day hardly speaking,
At night, mutual and experienced torturers.
Libby, our principal weapon,
spun helplessly between us.

'Don't take your venom out on the child!'
Frank would yell at me.
Then whisk her out in his M.G.
To the zoo. To the park.
One day he brought her back
bloodied by a swing.
It was late. Dark.
I didn't say anything.
Called the doctor. Made bandages.
Filled up on whisky.

Later on, both drunk,
he threw me down the cellar stairs
'Slut!' he kept shouting.
'Slovenly, drunken bitch!'
Which was close to the truth.
I never could live with my life
unless I was drunk.
I never could sleep or cry
until I was drunk.
I drank all day.

One week Frank went away . . .
just one of his conferences . . .
and Libby came down with 'flu. A fever.
But she wasn't that sick.
Just sick enough to slash nerves into strips.
Moaning and vomiting
whining and bullying . . .
Panic like a hornet in my brain.
Even my diet of whisky couldn't keep me sane.
No. Don't you tell me she's only a baby.
You know as well as I do, dear,
that babies have selfish grown
bitch personalities curled up in them . . .
like molars or hair.
When she screamed
she knew she made me scream.
And when I screamed,
she knew I screamed guilt.
Mother! Can't you feel what I felt?
I had to get out of there.
For her sake. For her sake. I . . .
Mother, I wished she would die.

So I slept myself sober.
Installed my crone baby-sitter.
Drove to the station.
Took the first train.

It was one of those days when
April is like October. Rain
through a wind full of
knife-edged, excitable sunlight.

Walking from Central Station
feeling slenderer, blonder . . .
familiar shiver of pleasure when
men stopped to stare.
Sky again! Younger.

Too scared to go to bars . . .
wandering like a schoolgirl from
museum to museum . . .

The Modern Art. The Guggenheim.
The Frick. The Metropolitan.
At the end, in the end
to the Cloisters.
You took me there often as a child,
you remember? Your small puzzled
prudish fat daughter!

But weirdly mother, weirdly,
this time it was just as before.
Just as hallowed and hushed and mysterious.
Just as drenched in its greyness and gentleness.
As if I'd been waiting there somewhere . . .
some part of me waiting in childhood,
expecting myself to come back.

There was one chapel . . .
could I have dreamed it?
Crouched, resigned, half-caryatids,
shouldering the arches like sins . . .
on the altar, stiff, under a baldachin,
a statue, a crude wooden Mary
dangling her homunculus son.

She was worn, wormeaten,
hunched in the vestiges of drapery,
Her features? Weary.
Weary and purposeless with suffering.
Her face? Void. A wound of
perpetual suffering.

And she stared at me, down at me,
suffering, out of one
glazed terrible eye.
I took in that gaze like a blade!

What was it? A threat or a lie?
Or did she know?
Her thin Christ had no head!
But did she know?

I don't know what I did,
or why. It blurs now, but I
woke up to find myself here
where they've taken my belt and my
wedding ring, where they
specialize in keeping me weeping.

Come when you can, or when
the whitecoats let you.
But they may not let you, of course.
They think you're to blame.
Good God, mother, I'm not insane!
How can I get out of here?
Can't you get me out of here?

I'll try, I'll try, really,
I'll try again. The marriage.
The baby. The house. The whole damn bore!

Because for me what the hell else is there?
Mother, what more? What more?

Anna Adams

(53) UNRECORDED SPEECH

She says 'How was you?' Kissing. 'Come on in,
I'm all of a muck-sweat, having a merry-go-round;
you've caught me doing my work.'
She doesn't clean, but circumvents the dirt.
Chairs stand on tables – 'All of a tizz-wozz.'
(Has that been spelt before?) 'A lick of paint,'
she says, propping her brush in turps,
'freshens things up a bit.' She paints the door
and skirting-boards; washes white window-veils.
Houses, bedsitters, flats, extend herself.
She makes the best of it, but likes a move;
it's like a change of dress, changing address.
I've lost count of the changes. 'Home at last!'
is said too often to be credible.
We'll write it on her tomb, or jar of ash,
unless she sees us out.
She says 'The poor old lady,' of someone
no older than herself.
'She's gone a bit – you know dear – gone a bit
doo-lally. Poor old thing. It takes all sorts – '
From childhood she remembers sparkling frost,
and walking out in it in Christmas clothes –
a coat her mother made her – vivid mauve –
'so bright against the snow.'
'And of a Friday afternoon
the teacher read to us. That was the best.'
Stories have been essential food since then.
Peg's Paper, H.E. Bates, Hardy and all
except romances; 'that don't interest me.'
She fills her days 'somehow', since Hubby died,
but she has grown since then.
'All in a lifetime dear,' she says of death.
Her words may be dead language soon;
that's why I write them down. They will be heard
'never no more', as she said at the birth

of my husband, her only child,
proving that double negatives mean 'No'.

HER DANCING DAYS

Or the Death of Mantovani Set Her Off (54)

Those old tunes take me back. I used to go
to dances every Saturday. Of course
I wasn't never going to give it up,
and nor was Lily Cannon, but we did.
We wasn't taught, we just picked up the steps.
In Summer there was dances in Brent Park;
they called them 'flannel dances': out of doors.
The men could wear grey flannels, not the girls.
I used to make my dresses, buy the stuff
up Cricklewood, and sew them in a day.
I liked the winter-evening dances best,
and used to dance with Horace – he was tall,
and we danced well together – Percival –
he was a butler, rather serious –
Jack Roach, Jack Young, and I forget who else;
but there was one I used to like, and then
one Saturday he wasn't there, and I
was heartbroke. Then he wrote.
I was to meet him at the Bald Faced Stag
one Sunday afternoon. We'd never met
by day. I didn't like the looks of him.
And Horace was engaged. Then, at a fair
with Lil, she was all out for a good time,
we met these two. One of them wore a cap.
I don't like caps. 'I'll have him then,' said Lil:
all four slid down the helter-skelter, then
the heel come off me shoe; I had to hop;
he fixed it for me. Later, we arranged
to meet again next evening at the Hyde.
    Lily come round, and sat down by the fire

to knit. 'I'm going out,' I said; 'You're not,
it's raining.' But I was. I had to go.
We didn't know each other's names,
or where we worked, or anything.
And there he waited for me, in the wet,
and fifty years began.
   I said I'd never give up dancing, and
he said the same of football, but we did;
and Lily gave up dancing too, quite soon.
   We was both seventeen.

Elaine Feinstein

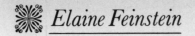

CALLIOPE IN THE LABOUR WARD (55)

she who has no love for women
married and housekeeping

now the bird notes begin
in the blood in the June morning
look how these ladies are
as little squeamish as
men in a great war

have come into their bodies
as their brain dwindles to
the silver circle on
eyelids under sun
and time opens
pain in the shallows to wave up and over them

grunting in gas and air
they sail to a
darkness without self
where no will reaches

in that abandon less
than human
give birth
bleak as a goddess

THE MEDIUM (56)

My answer would have to be music
which is always deniable, since in my
silence, which you question, is only a landscape

of water, old trees and a few irresolute
birds. The weather is also inconstant.
Sometimes the light is golden, the leaves unseasonable.

And sometimes the ice is red, and the moon
hangs over it, peeled, like a Chinese fruit.
I am sorry not to be more articulate.

When I try, the words turn ugly as rats and
disorder everything, I cannot be quiet,
I want so much to be quiet and loving

If only you wanted that. My sharpest thoughts
wait like assassins always in the dry wheat. They
chat and grin. Perhaps you should talk to them?

(57) PATIENCE

In water nothing is mean. The fugitive
enters the river, she is washed free;
her thoughts unravel like weeds of
green silk: she moves downstream
as easily as any cold-water creature

can swim between furred stones, brown
fronds, boots and tins the river holds equally.
The trees hiss overhead. She feels their shadows.
She imagines herself clean as a fish,
evasive, solitary, dumb. Her prayer:
to make peace with her own monstrous nature.

(58) JUNE

Dried up old cactus
   yellowing in several limbs
sitting on my kitchen window
   I'd given you up for dead
but you've done it again overnight
   with a tasselled trumpet flower

and a monstrous blare of red!
   So it's June, June again, hot sun
birdsong and dry air;
   we remember the desert
and the cities where grass is rare.
   Here by the willow-green river
we lie awake in the terrace
   because it's June, June again;
nobody wants to sleep
   when we can rise through beech trees
unknown and unpoliced
   unprotected veterans
abandoning our chores
   to sail out this month in nightgowns
as red and bold as yours:
   because it's June, June again.
Morning will bring birdsong
   but we've learnt on our bodies
how each Summer day is won
   from soil, the old clay soil
and that long, cold kingdom.

COASTLINE (59)

This is the landscape of the Cambrian age:
      shale, blue quartz, planes of slate streaked with
iron and lead; soapstone, spars of calcite;
      in these pools, fish are the colour of sand,
velvet crabs like weeds, prawns transparent as water.

This shore was here before man. Every tide
      the sea returns, and floats the bladderwrack,
The flower animals swell and close over creatures
      rolled-in, nerveless, sea-food, fixed and forgotten.

My two thin boys balance on Elvan Stone
    bent-backed, intent, crouched with their string and pins,
their wet feet white, lips salt, and skin wind-brown,
    watching with curiosity and compassion:
further out, Time and Chance are waiting to happen.

(60) THE MAGIC APPLE TREE

Sealed in rainlight one
November sleepwalking afternoon streets
I remembered Samuel Palmer's garden
Waterhouse in Shoreham, and at once
I knew: that the chill of wet
brown streets was no more literal
than the yellow he laid there against
his unnatural blue because
together they worked upon me like
an icon   infantine

he called his vision / so it was
with the early makers of icons, who
worked humbly, choosing wood without resin.
They stilled their spirits before using the gold
and while the brightness held under the kvass
their colours too induced
the peculiar joy of abandoning restlessness

and now in streets where only white
mac or car metal catches the falling
light, if we sing of
the red and the blue and the texture of goat hair,
there is no deceit in our prophecy:
for even now our brackish waters can
be sweetened by a strange tree.

Ruth Fainlight

ANOTHER FULL MOON

Another full moon. I knew without checking
The date or the almanac. Again I am
Tearful, uncertain, subdued and oppressed.
It becomes more an abasement each time to
Acknowledge I still respond, anachronistic
As an astrolabe, reliable as
Litmus paper. No hope of escape, though I
Should much prefer not to be absolutely
In thrall to the rhythm of ocean and
Cosmos, so solemnly primitive, such a
Mantic pauper. With her roughened tongue, the moon
Curdles my milk of human kindness; her
Maniac yellow eye glares through the curtains
And follows every movement. Her purpose is
Obscure, random and cruel. It is worse than
Being a prisoner, because between her
Appearances I forget how she rules me:
How her gauntleted hand crushes the back of my
Neck, forcing me lower, making me grovel,
Ridiculous and awful as a manticore.
I wonder if this is the only way
Possible: if it must be true that there
Will never be room for wit or humour
In the universe we share, and for all
My days I shall bear the scars of her torture,
Marked forever as her creature and her fool.

THE OTHER

Whatever I find if I search will be wrong.
I must wait: sternest trial of all, to contain myself,
Sit passive, receptive, and patient, empty
Of every demand and desire, until
That other, that being I never would have found

Though I spent my whole life in the quest, will step
Clear of the shadows, approach like a wild, awkward child.

And this will be the longest task: to attend,
To open myself. To still my energy
Is harder than to use it in any cause.
Yet surely she will only be revealed
By pushing against the grain of my ardent nature
That always yearns for choice. I feel it painful
And strong as a birth in which there is no pause.

I must hold myself back from every lure of action
To let her come closer, a wary smile on her face,
One arm lifted: to greet me or ward off attack –
I cannot decipher that uncertain gesture.
I must even control the pace of my breath
Until she has drawn her circle near enough
To capture the note of her faint reedy voice.

And then as in dreams, when a language unspoken
Since times before childhood is recalled (when
I was as timid as she, my forgotten sister –
Her presence my completion and reward), I begin
To understand, in fragments, the message she waited
So long to deliver. Loving her I shall learn
My own secret at last from the words of her song.

Jenny Joseph

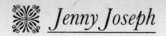

THE LOST CONTINENT (63)

A thread of silver marks along the sand
The shallow start of the deep ocean. Dry
Among the dunes a rusty cable points
Two fingers to the white and morning air.
All messages that travel to the land,
Crowded with houses and listening people
Whose life means words, are cut off here, and wander,
Not even sounding, on the empty shore:
The wire no longer murmurs with the noise
That would be words were they interpreted.

Deep within that ocean lies my love.
Once it was linked through every rib of sand
That ran along the bottom to the shore;
And every ripple and every fish that waved
Its tail between the centre and headland
Echoed in green fields. Wrecks became fossils,
The land changed face and we upon the land,
But still the ocean cable reached its home.

But now even near the land sea bed is strange,
Never approached even on calm days
When clearly you could see what lies there.
No word has passed, no tremor felt for years.
The great fish swim unnoticed and the channels
Silt up and shift and make no difference.
The elements are alien and separate.

Sleeping deep like a child within the womb
The curled-up figure of the woman lies
And lost within that passive sea my words.

DOG BODY AND CAT MIND (64)

The dog body and cat mind
Lay in the room with the fire dying.
Will went out and locked the door.

Then the dog started howling.
He went to the door and scratched at it.
He went to the window and barked at it.
He prowled round the room sniffing and whining
Put his nose to the wainscot and whimpered in the dust.
The dog body and the cat mind
Locked in a room with the fire dying
And the dog would not lie down and be still.

He hurtled his shoulders against the wall;
He upset the cat's food and stepped in it.
He barked hard at his wild reflection
In the blank window. And banged his head
Until it ached, on the stone floor,
And still could not lie down and be still.

Then worn out with howling
And scratching and banging the dog flopped
To a weary defeated sleep.

And then the cat got up and started walking.

(65) ROSE IN THE AFTERNOON

Not rose of death:
Drawing in to your centre each wave of colour
That your arrested petals give to the air –
Dying inwardly the petals do not fall.

Nor rose of heaven:
Calm at the centre of this city
Monstrous moons, exuberance of stars
Have nothing to do with the light that you collect.
The light of the world has nourished your cut bloom
Drop by drop drawn down into your blood
As drop by drop your root took life from the ground.

Far down the river a cork popples the water
The motion quivers and rocks the air until

Rose in my room you catch and turn the movement
Mote by mote absorbed into your flesh
The vibrant morning tide within your veins.
Equally, hands moving in shuttered clubs
Though no light enters there to give time progress,
Flick flash-ringed fingers as red five black queen
Fall. Seeping through streets this gleam feeds you.

Day by day you calcify, embalming
The vigour you exhale. Fragile you have
Subdued the molten morning in your calyx
The palpitating golden fire that poured
Over the ridges of buildings, right angles, volutes;
And converted percussion of day to this calm strong
 flowing
Light lapping gentle round the afternoon;
Will equally subdue the night to come –
A ray shooting the dark – into a mere
Closure of a known twilight, not different state.

O rose in the afternoon, your only movement
The imperceptible falling in your blood,
Your vibrant stillness more speaking than all the voices,
If I could give you as answer, my sentence your statement
I would be dumb in peace with the light gone
And only your image waking in the dark.

BACK TO BASE (66)

Mole who knows,
Who burrows up for air
Sniffs, intoxicated, so much fresh stuff:
River smell, green of leaves; sniffs space
Feels (heady) the air, feels space swirl round,
Senses (he cannot see) that stars beyond
Beyond what he could ever want or think of

Reel and hold sway behind the dark up there.
That dark is far enough – a thin dark
Not like this, familiar, close to pelt
Holding him.

And mole returning in time before the world swoops
Perhaps a little after the point danger might come
And the light break and trap him and bludgeon him;
Mole missing the ether, creeps to his place:
Close corridors he does not need to see.
Weeps for the stars and space and fresh green smell
The river moving by mysteriously
He does not know, but knows something is there
Stream where others flourish, that others can use,
Weeps, but how comforting the smell of earth
How truly right his own dark; basement
Where the bend
Cuts out the ruinous light
The brittle noises, laughter of thundering horses
And suchlike hysterical creatures.
Round the next bend, and the low breathing
Of his own life and all his life around him
Imperceptible in the upper air, receives him
Concentrated positive and tangible.
Mole he sleeps deep, his velvet nurtured by
The proper dryness, cohesion, in the earth
His only place, he knows,
Safe from the pull of the malign dews of the stars
The vast cold glitter, thin twanging in the spheres
That draws men, crazy, across shadeless tundra.

Frances Horovitz

THE WOMAN'S DREAM (67)

A man and woman
alone in a vast sea,
companions of the water
swimming in grave delight.

They have forgotten the tree-fringed shore,
cannot imagine underfoot
pebbles or broken shell.
No looming rock, or fin or sail,
        or musky isle
disturb their calm.
The sea upholds them, shapes them;
their fragile plash scarce breaks its skin.

Their first sun rises,
spills at the sea's edge,
patterns the spread silk.
The man is all gold.
He gasps, he shimmers,
tosses up metallic drops,
his arms flash like swords.
He is robed and crowned in gold.
'To the sun,' he calls, 'Come.'

The sun does not finger her;
the sea would whisper her in all oceans,
would speak through each orifice.
Currents probe at her thigh,
her blood is slower than tides,
a tongue of water has entered her throat.
She flails, falls back in shadow,
is succoured by sea-beasts –
dolphin, whale.
Summoned from unfathomable dark
they rise beneath her,
her belly flexed to the dolphin's curve.
She is borne, streaming,
into the miraculous, hurting air.

She does not turn to watch
where he, unmoving now,
is drowned, subsumed, in light.

(68) THE MESSENGER

Every five years the Thracians chose by lot a messenger to tell the gods of their needs. They sent him thus: three spears were held firm, the chosen man flung up into the air to fall on the spears. If he died the gods were favourable; if not, they sent another man.

in a spathe of silence
he moves
treading on worn stone,
what he was
herdsman, lover
he has forgotten,
self, like dross
sifted in the running stream

his skin no longer contains him
the subtle bones of his skull
move apart
out of his eyes he sees
only shadows
through white air
his spine
an avalanche of light

hands hover,
touch
what he no longer is

a huge flower opens
tremulous,
sky blooms;

parabola beyond eagles
lazy, infinite;
in his mind
periphery of dark,
the white curve
dispersing to zero

spears run like flame on water

on flung hills
an eagle descends

MOON (69)

city bred
        I watch the moon
                through glass

distorted beyond vagary
        she rides
                the accuser
swinging tides
like recalcitrant skirts

her solitude breeds memory
heaves it to birth
mocks the still-born

moon, I remember –
your light a scalpel thrust
from a mouth of white bone

even through glass
I mirror your loneliness
walking in warm rooms

– sometimes I wish you
no more than a thumbprint
on the edge of the sky

Penelope Shuttle

(70) GONE IS THE SLEEPGIVER

Gone is the sleepgiver,
softly, mildly,
gone into the early rain,
leaving me
with the loneliness of the day
when I must empty rubbish from the baskets,
mend clothes, sort cupboards,
invent feasts:
gone is the sleepgiver,
leaving me the crude colours of life,
the too-bright treasures of the day

(oh but in my dream
I was losing strength,
or being turned into a bird).

(71) LOCALE

Should I know this room,
this stunned firmament?

Outside, a bedridden climate,
rain, cloud, undrinkable dark

Always this wrong weather
draws me down into its poverty,

strips me of all but weariness
Should I know this room?

Yes, I've seen those ceiling cracks before,
this is the room of all that is unfinished

No mirrors on the wall,
for here no woman is fair

How familiar it seems,
how short a time since my last visit,

the furniture is frosted with dust,
the bedding is damp,

the room is unlit,
dark as the raw weather

and I – I am held prisoner here,
captive between the belly of one dark
and the thigh of another . . .

so what will free me,
unlock the door of this slum?

Only bitter and wise blood,
the shorn fleece of the womb.

MARITIMES (72)

Sunlight in the house
and the rooms
calm ships anchored
in a supple vapour.

The maze of summer unwinds
and my maritimes begin.
It is the sea that remains
after all else has been tried.

It is the sea.

Through half-closed eyes
I watch the ocean, its ancestry.
Many of those faces resemble mine,
frowning, smiling . . .

Jump under the wave, they say,
jump under . . .

Beneath the wave I am going, then,
big with child.

And in this sea there is to be no drowning.
Amid these waves
no suffocation.

I go into the ocean, and rock there,
just as my child turns
on the waterwheel of me,
held in a web of moon,
fed on the salt and blood of me.

(73) EARLY PREGNANCY

18th May 1976

Almost sheer fatigue
and yet a steadfastness

A life is simmering in me,
brewing, distilling in me

Rough weather and its sweet messages
bolt and skid outside

I watch, tired and heavy
but standing on the tips of my toes,
peering over the weather

My old self peels off, old-fashioned ghost,
like fine rain, or a filched song

I am moving towards my newness,
the life that is beyond weather
growing strong in me

Stormfree runner soon to rise
out of the ancient climate of the womb

EXPECTANT MOTHER (74)

In the stillness,
uterine,
hidden from me,
hidden from mirrors,
the foetal roots of wrist
and heart
are coiled within me.
They belong to the child,
to the incast,
a plumage of constellations.

I walk around the house
in bare feet
and a warm rope of blood
links me to my child

Rain falls on gardens and inscriptions
but I hold the edge of the rain.
I am a receptacle
in which other rain, amniotic, gathers,
for the one in his official residence
to enjoy.

I think of the quiet use of the unborn eyelids
and the stillness of my breasts that swell up,
a warm procedure of strength.

Already a name suggests its syllables,
but this remains secret,
a fishtail shadow,
a whisper between the night and the day.

Vivienne Finch

(75) GREEN ICE

What new responsibilities are we hatching now
what fresh green does my heart mint
to be finger-smudged   by you
                        across my breasts

hands touch   yet remain
tiny collections of independent bone
        filled   by invisible gifts
your fingers unnerve my flesh
resolve me   into merging pain
with forms the body-questions take

but this is the first time
without words of love
which are replaced by 'do you like . . . ?'
                        or 'do you want . . . ?'
queries which are not fertilized
as we diminish into kisses, into pillows,
into the frozen frame: uncertainty

you give me your throat to taste
you give me 'green'
the dreadful pressure of green
you forbid me to regret
you make me listen inwards

only to hear a glacier   shift a little
knowing the rules
but not how to defeat them
(such an oblique kind of wisdom)

so aware of the verb 'to love'
yet not even allowed to whisper
one of its many conjugations

you come to me and make me green
entering with no ringing bells
entering where the soul may be
the part of you that sees the dream

and this contemplation
of slow entering is nowhere
near perfection

for though our mouths make promises
that nothing comes of nothing
and your palm gestures peace
across my body:

we are vulnerable

wondering when gold will join that green
or when the level of a single absence
will recede below the vision's tide

this friendship is not accurate
is too involved with slipping
unobserved into my head
where words are temporized by amber

we have been host to many other pains
cannot afford misunderstanding

thus the questions and the questioning
the verbal double helix
linking impulse to emotion

maybe my eyes will shed their dying stars
but you will never quite be near enough
to catch their falling glitter

only your shadow will lie calmly
by my side as we lean back
appearing to reach sleep

with silence as a body-question
still unfertilized

inside these green walls of normality
where there are Druids
rustling in the leaves.

(76) INERTIA

this morning, the memory of you
dissolves like breath on glass

dissolves like sleek cold fish
into your mouth's dark estuary

dissolves like warmth to frost
heart to no beating
no movement
ice

not shocked into rigidity
like walls who see too much,
but shifted to a permanent curve,

a sorrowing,
like arms folding around emptiness,
knowing no warmth,

until memory is quite separate
from speech – remote
and isolated in its field of ice,

rebounding from the coldness
like echoes from walls,

water
turning to ice
on fingers

to add yet another dimension
to flesh – one more barrier
between touching

that is not meltwater
nor the chasm,

but the iceberg
that will not dissolve,

that freezes words to its tip,
or strands the growth
of this still morning
to its heavy flow,

that can freeze
into no deeper silence,

no sadder smile
to reflect sorrow,

can dissolve no further.

Marina Tsvetayeva

(77) *From* THE POEM OF THE END

(Translated from the Russian by Elaine Feinstein)

1

A single post, a point of rusting
  tin in the sky
marks the fated place we
  move to, he and I

on time   as death is
  prompt   strangely
too smooth the gesture of
  his hat to me

menace at the edges of his
  eyes   his mouth tight
shut   strangely too low is the
  bow he makes tonight

on time? that false note in
  his voice, what
is it the brain alerts to and the
  heart drops at?

under the evil sky, that sign of
  tin and rust.
Six o'clock. There he is waiting
  by the post.

Now we kiss soundlessly, his
  lips stiff as
hands are given to queens, or
  dead people thus

round us the shoving of elbows of
  ordinary bustle
and strangely irksome rises the
  screech of a whistle

howls like a dog screaming
  angrier, longer: what
a nightmare strangeness life is
  at death point

and that nightmare reached my waist
  only last night
and now reaches the stars, it has
  grown to its true height

crying silently love love until
  – Has it gone
six, shall we go to the cinema?
  I shout it! home!

8

Last bridge   I won't
give up or take out my hand
this is the last bridge
the last bridging between

water   and firm land:
and I am saving these
coins for death
for Charon, the price of Lethe

this   shadow money
from my dark hand I press
soundlessly into
the shadowy darkness of his

shadow money it is
no gleam and tinkle in it
coins for shadows:
the dead have enough poppies

This bridge

Lovers for the most
part are without hope: passion
also is just
a bridge, a means of connection

It's warm: to nestle
close at your ribs, to move in
a visionary pause
towards nothing, beside nothing

no   arms no   legs
now, only the bone of my
side is alive where
it presses directly against you

life in that side
only, ear and echo is it: there
I stick like white to
egg yolk, or an eskimo to his fur

adhesive, pressing
joined to you: Siamese
twins are no nearer.
The woman you call mother

when she forgot
all things in motionless triumph
only to carry you:
she did not hold you closer.

Understand: we have
grown into one as we slept and
now I can't jump
because I can't let go your hand

and I won't be torn off
as I press close to you: this
bridge is no husband
but a lover: a just slipping past

our support: for the
river is fed with bodies!
I bite in like a tick
you must tear out my roots to be rid of me

like ivy   like a tick
inhuman   godless
to throw me away like a thing, when there is

no thing I ever prized
in this empty world of things.
Say this is only dream,
night still and afterwards morning

an express   to Rome?
Granada? I won't know myself
as I push off
the Himalayas of bedclothes.

But this dark is deep:
now I warm you with my blood, listen
to this flesh.
It is far truer than poems.

If you are warm, who
will you go to tomorrow for that?
This is delirium,
please say this bridge cannot

end
        as it ends.

Nicki Jackowska

(78) FAMILY OUTING – A CELEBRATION

And I took myself for a walk in the woods that day
all ten yards of me, family and all
All of my dear old aunts shuffling in the leaves
and my sister, married now, out on parole
And I took my wives and my daughters, carrying provisions
(in case the sun might hurt) under the green leaves
And my father, with his stern blue eye
and the ancient poodle, gone grey, between us all.
Gran, bringing up the rear, the arch-surrogate
My mother's white shoes flashed in the sun
The luggage that was carried by everyone
would sink a liner, certainly it submerged me.

But the sun was bright, Aunt Alice sprightly
I knew Gran had fresh cucumber sandwiches
tucked in her bag. I told the family not to lag
but keep together, in case of accidents.
We didn't want all of that gnarled old tree
spilling its marrow, for all the world to see.
Sometimes the path vanished beneath the ferns
and father called upon to redirect us all
would puff and blow at all the energy
needed to decide, under the blinding light
of mother's white suit and equally white
and blinding quality of mind. In the end

He charged in one direction, scattering the aunts
whose china ornaments didn't stand a chance
against such sudden choice; my mother's voice
was heard among the cows three fields away
The family, in sudden disarray, without identity
fell like a pack of cards upon the wind
and needed several minutes of a precise kind
to close ranks against the nosy, scattering breeze.
I picked up Aunt Mathilda's carrier-bag and mittens
and Gran's clean pressed linen handkerchieves

dusted the loose earth from Doris's floral dress
and rescued Uncle Jack from the carpet of damp leaves.

The path was narrowing now, and cheek by jowl
we squeezed beneath the nettles and the thorns
clinging together in tottering whimsical support.
Without a thought, I saw the grisly snarling fangs
of some old beast of prey among the undergrowth
But no-one noticed, only father seemed to dig his heels
harder in the mud, and mother's brand-new suit
was stained with grass and tea from her reluctant tasks
and all the flying insects in their mad assault
upon her, as she shone forth like an old bronze mask.
I should have worn my plastic mac, she said
and Jack said, here's mine, you only have to ask.

Gran was guardian of that particular roundabout
Her iron will pressed down upon the nearest bough
which burst to let the assorted family through.
The shadow of no name was snapping at her heels
as every night he prowled the brown linoleum
of Gran's dark stair, and caught me watching there
under the raven moon, the starless, careful night.
I wished the poppies and the cornflower blue
of father's eyes, and mother's clean white lawns.
And soon the ancient poodle fell down dead
and mother wept as though it had been him
My father's arms and legs were very thin.

It seemed the passing of that canine life
unpicked the seams holding the party fast
And so the great disaster came at last
letting the thunders loose, the pricks and spoils.
Mathilda cut across the fields for home
and vanished in the grasses; tired though he was
my father carried in addition all of my mother
almost smothering her; and Gran, though strong
began a winding down of her most constant song.

To cut a story short (by almost half a life)
they fell like harvest-corn, long over-ripe
into their caverns, into their haunted rooms,

Leaving mine empty, the clean scythe in my hands.

(79) THE INSECT KITCHEN

Is the clock wound up, is it wound?
he said,
waving his bandaged fist
Round the table he stalked her
his gunmetal head wrapped in linen

You with your jaws, your jaws
you eating up all my words
like a great daft sheep
like a penny machine
like a heifer, she muttered

Has the cat been fed, been fed
with the shreds of supper?
he whispered,
and lapped at her silky legs
and the pipes freezing

You with your centipede heart
and trying to net me
she hissed,
and the milk boiling

Wrap up the tablecloth
and bind my head
Patch up the walls
I'll play knives with you
now all the family's
safe in bed, she said

Is the curtain pulled, is it pulled?
he croaked,
his breath like a sliver of glass,
And the spider shakes in its corner
the webs all alight
the marigolds falling

Five times round the table
his eye rolling, they prance
among the parsley, the petals,
the garlic, the ironing-board

Soon her old grey cardigan lay
like a rag on the floor
and her skirt was over her head
as he did the round once more

THE SISTERS (80)

And I made myself a surrogate wedding-day
bought a few scraps of lurex, and a tin of salmon
a set of lace mats from the bric-a-brac shop
a feather or two, and a plastic arum lily

and she sat in the park where the old house was
where the ruins paved the way to happiness
the last storm had torn a tree through the heart

The light was thick and keen, the cake shone
I stitched the silver-threaded cloth in bunches
on my fat hips and sugared my heavy lips
The radio voice said we may expect thunder

and the roses shone like beacons in the dust
and all the window ledges eaten with rust
she picked her way by starlight between stones

Someone had dropped cherry-juice on the lace
I pinned it to my hair, a creamy ring
of arcane light. Well into the night
I folded tinfoil round two dozen cardboard bells

and in the morning, laid like an old maid
upon her work, the new light flickered in vain
She stared among the ruins and the broken cake
The lace fell like swans' feathers over the lake

(81) THE MEETING

He opened the car door. There was a low rumble
which could have been my heart or could have been
the engine breathing. Or could have been the
distant thrust of a lorry bringing supplies to the
end of england. He stood holding the door.
I stood and listened to unimaginable insects in the
nearby grass and rolled my warmness among the stems
and blades and fragrances. I walked the ten paces
to the car. Inside was hot and fierce. It was
summer.

He opened the car door and his arms flung wide
like great wings of a preying bird. It seemed he
wore an opaque and unusually vivid shirt which
clamoured for attention like market stalls and
birdwings. The trousers were grey and soft like a
mole. I liked his menagerie. The hills opened.
I praised the grand opening bars of this sonata
lost among west country lanes. The threads of such
a morning were held in a tight skein. Later I could
replace my steps while the scarlet upholstery was too
hot like the breath of a stone.

He opened the car door in parenthesis. The event
was of no significance. We met at the station at

three forty-two and exchanged timetables. His hands
lay in his pockets. They only came out to open the
car door. A man and a woman fled across the tarmac
like two refugees from warfare. He entered the car
at the same time as I – perfect parallel lines.
Immaculate guests at a convention, slicing the territory
of love precisely into two halves.

He opened the car door and his shirts fell softly
so that I dared not interrupt them. There is no
interfering with falling stars. In the dying season
he was grey and camouflaged. No soldier and no gun.
Only a fallen woman he mourned for. So I crept to
the car and squeezed past the ghost who guarded the
door. The one who looked out of his eyes.

He opened the car door, his face written with many
births and the folds of departures. Between one
moment and the next, a bridge built and bombed. The
world fought and died in its jungle, while we read
the several histories calligraphed in a diminutive
hand on the metal door-frame. The life not yet
invented.

Frankie Armstrong

(82) OUT OF THE DARKNESS

Out of the darkness comes the fear of
what's to come
Out of the darkness comes the dread of
what's undone.
Out of the darkness comes the hope that
we can run
And out of the darkness comes the
knowledge of the sun.

Out of the darkness comes the fear of
the unknown
Out of the darkness comes the dread of
bleaching bone.
Out of the darkness comes the hope we're
not alone
And out of the darkness grow the seeds
that we have sown.

Out of the darkness come the fear revenge and hate
Out of the darkness comes the dread
of indifferent fate
Out of the darkness comes the hope
we're not too late
And out of the darkness comes the songs
that we create.

Darkness is the place of birth –
darkness is the womb.
Darkness is the place of rest – darkness is
the tomb.
Death belongs to life – half of day is night
The end won't come in darkness but a
blinding flash of light.

MONTH OF JANUARY (83)

It was in the month of January the hills
were clad in snow,
It was over hills and valleys my true
love he did go.
It was there I spied a pretty fair maid
with a salt tear in her eye;
She had a baby in her arms and
bitter she did cry.

Oh cruel was my father who barred
the door on me.
And cruel was my mother this
dreadful sight to see.
And cruel was my own true love who
changed his mind for gold.
And cruel was the winter's night
that pierced my heart with cold.

For the higher up the palm tree
grows the sweeter is the bark
And the fairer that a young man speaks
the falser is his heart.
He will kiss you and embrace you till
he thinks he has you won,
Then he'll go away and leave you all
for some other one.

So come all you pretty fair young maids
a warning take by me
And never try and build your nest
At the top of a high tree.
For the leaves they all will
wither and the branches will decay
And the beauty of a fine young man will all soon fade away.

(*Traditional Irish*)

(84) THE COLLIER LASS

My name's Polly Parker I come o'er
from Worseley,
My mother and father work down the
coal mine,
Our family is large, we have got seven children,
so I am obliged to work down the
same mine.
As this is my fortune, I know you'll feel
sorry,
That in such employment my days
I must pass,
But I keep up my spirits, I sing
and look cheerful,
Although I am but a poor collier lass.

By the greatest of dangers each
day I'm surrounded:
I hang in the air by a rope or a chain.
The mine may give in – I may be
killed or wounded
Or perish by damp or the fire of
a flame.
But what would you do if it weren't
for our labours?
In greatest starvation your days you
would pass,
For we would provide you with life's
greatest blessing,
So do not despise a poor collier lass.

All the day long you may say
we are buried,
Deprived of the light and the warmth
of the sun.
And often at nights from our bed we
are hurried,

The water is in and barefoot we run.
But though we go ragged and black
are our faces,
As kind and as free as the best we'll
be found
And our hearts are more white than
your lords in high places,
Although we're poor colliers that
work underground.

I'm growing up fast – somehow
or another
There's a young collier lad strangely
runs through my mind.
And in spite of the talking of father
and mother,
I think I should marry if he is inclined.
But should he prove surly and will
not befriend me,
another and better chance may come to pass.
And my friends here I know to him
will commend me
And I'll be no longer a poor collier
lass.

(*Industrial Broadside*)

WOMEN OF MY LAND (85)

Down streams of centuries grown old,
Across the seas of time,
You wove your love and hopes and fears
Into tune and rhyme.

Chorus
And now I try and sing your song
And hope to understand

Who I am, and who you were
Women of my land.

You spun your sufferings into song
To help you to survive
In factories and farms and mines
To keep your soul alive.

And sometimes children brought you joy
But often brought you pain
For lovers left and you could find
No shelter from your shame.

At evenings when the Spring was young
You sang wild songs of love
And called your lover far or near
A blackbird or a dove.

Your songs could tell a crafty tale
Full of laughter and wit
You turned the tables on the men
And the biter found himself bit.

And some of you were bold as brass
Said to hell with custom and law
And dressed as sailor and soldier boys
You went off to war.

Together you sang in farm and factories
Arm in arm as you strolled down the street
Your voices rang; on the picket line you sang
In time to the tramp of your feet.

And always they said your place was to serve
Husband, master and king
You tried to defy this centuries-old lie
And one of your ways was to sing.

And when I think how many of you died
So young in labour and pain
These songs I sing are the tribute that I bring
And make me a link in your chain.

The Renaming

POETRY COMING FROM THE WOMEN'S LIBERATION MOVEMENT 1970–80

Introduction

and they ransacked her streets and cities
trees and sunlight and leaves

and straining to keep awake at night
and make the darkness her own
she named the moon and stars
and called the night sea
                    the night sea

to help
        let her be
                    still

Valerie Sinason (86)

I will sing high in the fire
my body her torch: oh let
the fierce goddess
come

Michele Roberts (88)

I have stood on the cliffs
with my thoughts without word
with the lines of the light
windstrokes that hammer
the air's wavering ridges with movement.
And you came from behind
and then saw that your hands
were clasped tight round my shoulders.
And a wingspread of cloud
rode bareback on the funnels of flame
and we stared at the sky.

Harriet Rose (89)

When the sun sets, here the crescent
rises – she sees neither,
having been a believer all her life, done
everything dutifully but one thing:
which was to remain behind her black seven veils
every living moment: to
take her flesh to sackcloth from birth
to death; to
keep their eyes clean
        for God, and his rigid kings and small fathers
on earth:
        she salaams down
on to, dear God, well trodden ground.

Judith Kazantzis (133)

A selection of poetry coming from the present-day women's liberation movement, or which could be said to share in the insights of feminism, now follows.

The fact that a poem has been included in this section rather than the preceding one, or vice versa, is not intended to suggest a rigid classification into work which is 'feminist' and work which is not. The areas of poetry which come primarily from a literary tradition, and poetry which is also shaped by specific political commitment as well as literary experience, overlap. However, poems shaped by a political commitment do, necessarily, have certain features in common.

As with the preceding section, choice of emphasis had to be made. The poetry here is only partly representative of feminist poetry as a whole. A great deal is being written within the present-day women's movement on the lines of the 'Rime of the Ancient Feminist', the 'Hermaphrodite's Song' and the 'Poem for Jacqueline Hill'. Work like this observes and reports in a very direct way on life and its meaning as many committed women experience it. Writing alone and in groups has a real meaning for many women today. Writing, for many of us, puts self-expression first and sets aside considerations of 'sounding like literature'. This is how it should be, for if all we could think about was the creation of literature many of us would never be able to start.

With this collection of poetry, though, the publishers and I found that what worked in the context of a collection that consisted largely of 'literary' material, was to use feminist material of some 'literary' quality. And this is what we have done. Space, of course, was a powerful consideration. A very large number of women write for pleasure and self-expression — and a very large number of them sent us manuscripts of real value which we were not able to represent here. I and the publishers would like to acknowledge all those who sent us manuscripts, and support them in continuing to develop as writers.

Many of the poets represented here are actively involved in feminist campaigns. Their work invites some comparisons with the women's rights campaigners represented in the second section. It may be that a greater variety of issues are examined in a more complex form in present-day 'feminist' writing: readers may make their own interpretations. It seems evident to me, however, that a central concern of present-day feminist writing is the act of naming, or rather, as Valerie Sinason (86) calls it, 'renaming'. Calling a spade a spade has never been a right that women can take for granted; morality, as well as literary criticism, has imposed severe constraints on what a 'lady' can safely say. Present-day women's writing, both the writing included here and all the rest that considerations of space have precluded, continually charts new territory. Women write in realistic ways about their Muse, who may well be themselves, about themselves as mothers and daughters and what that really means, the physical reality of their bodies, their sexuality, about what personal change is like, and how it illuminates the day-to-day experience of their lives. They write of old age and death. They write of spirituality – their language may shift from the male symbolic imagery of established religion to other imagery that tells the truth about their own spiritual experience. They may write of their own struggles and campaigns to change the quality of their life. Straightforward stuff maybe, but sign of an enormous shift when little more than a century ago convention decreed that women should write about hearts and flowers – old straw hats and old armchairs (see Eliza Cook) – if indeed they wrote at all. For women to begin to tell the truth about their lives, expansively and realistically, is not a small revolution.

As I read and re-read the work of the women who sent their manuscripts to me, or whose work I solicited, I became aware of similar themes running through the work of many of them. The body of work as a whole told a story. I have taken the decision to arrange the poems I have selected according to a few straightforward themes rather than chronologically or alphabetically. While aware that this approach may seem to smack of interpretation, I do believe that a poem is too often seen as an isolated fragment, that poetry as a whole originally sought to hand on a knowledge or tradition, and that, by assembling poems on similar themes together, we may gain something of a feeling of a knowledge which is shared.

What may be called 'Muse' poems introduce the sequence – poems of female identity, inspiration, creative power. The first goddess is the mother, and so there is a shift to poems of motherhood and family life. Motherhood may contain a divine meaning but it can also be a female role stereotype and an instrument of oppression. The woman experiencing this feels an intense need to change. But how, and to what? Life goes on, filled with both ordinary and extraordinary events, but, once the feminist context for perceiving it has been created, new and surprising meanings may constantly surface. The only option may now be to tell the truth about how things really are, to live with integrity. But what is the context in which personal experience is felt and recorded? The women's movement may support some women in the belief that the personal is political and that there is, therefore, a political meaning in what they previously perceived as personal experience. But there is too the wider context of women's oppression. This is experienced in a very immediate and painful way in physical violence against women. Women need to support each other in creating freedom, security and full self-expression for each other; a world that works for them – and for everyone. In the 'Poem for Jacqueline Hill', widely circulated through the winter of 1980/81 following the thirteenth (and final) murder by the so-called 'Yorkshire Ripper', Peter Sutcliffe, we hear the voice of Jacqueline Hill, Sutcliffe's last victim (138).

Let me be (you say)
Let me live in peace
Let my life be alright
Helpful to others, useful, a good life
I thought that was enough, (you say) that I was alright
How could it be me?
But it was me and I walked down
the dark road; never forget that, in your righteous rage:
for me, the death in darkness: to you, now, a hard dawn.

NOTE
The poems in this section are not grouped by poet, as they are in the previous sections. So a particular poet's work may be found at various points throughout the section.

The Poets

VALERIE SINASON (86) (104) (107). 'I was born in London in 1946, started writing poems and stories at the age of four and never stopped. So writing has always been a natural and important part of my life. I took an English degree, followed by a post-graduate teaching diploma in english and drama teaching. Writing and psychotherapy play a major part in my adult life. I find poetry-writing and therapy have important links as ways of seeking truth. I now work and train as a child psychotherapist, teach English literature and spend a fair amount of time giving poetry readings as well as writing. My poems have been published/broadcast/anthologised in such places as *One Foot on the Mountain* (1979), *Spare Rib, Contemporary Women Poets, Poetry Review, Tribune,* Thames Television, P.E.N., Arts Council anthologies, etc. Poetry theatre experience included being part of Prodigal Daughters, a women's poetry theatre group. I publish and edit *Gallery* magazine and am anxious to make sure women's poetry is properly represented in the small press world. I married in 1969 and have two children who enjoy writing poems!'

MICHELE ROBERTS (88) (100) (105) (111). Michele Roberts was born on 20 May 1949 in Bushey, Hertfordshire of a French mother and English father. She works as a poet, novelist, editor, teacher, journalist and reviewer. She is currently poetry editor for *City Limits.* She was co-author of *Cutlasses and Earrings* (1976), *Licking the Bed Clean* (1978), *Smile Smile Smile Smile* (1980) and the short-story anthology, *Tales I Tell My Mother* (1978). First novel, *A Piece of the Night,* was published in 1978. 'At the time of writing (January 1982) I am about to submit my second novel for publication. I've been writing since the age of five and have always wanted to be a writer. Writing for me is about exploring conflicts to do with self/world and imagining solutions, solving problems, healing splits. I couldn't live without writing. Much of my work so far has necessarily involved speaking with a gendered voice, examining images of the female self in order to integrate some, reject some, reinvent some, suggest new ones. All my work is about change . . . I live alone, cherish my privacy and solitude fiercely, and also depend a lot on the friendship network in which I move and which supports my life and gives me great joy and pleasure.'

HARRIET ROSE (89) (134) (137). Harriet Rose began writing as a young child and has appeared in numerous magazines and anthologies including *Ambit, Bananas, Confrontation, Word,* etc. Collections of poetry include *The Steel Circle, On Vultures, A Harsh Note in My Song* and *Purim Cycles* (forthcoming). Her last show, *Mellisandra,* was presented at the Hampstead Theatre Club in London and some of her fiction is in the Penguin Firebird Anthologies. 'I prefer writing surrealist poetry in unmeasured lines and developed a new criticism which I later discovered had been developed by Herbert Read, though I have developed it much further, adapting terminology from the performing arts. I have definite ideas about the spiritual end of poetics as well as the technical, preferring unfashionable rhetorical poets of the 1940s to constructionalist poets. On a personal level I am apolitical, painfully shy, and like a great deal of space around myself. I avoid large gatherings and parties when possible.'

MARY DORCEY (90) (99). Mary Dorcey was born in the Republic of Ireland in 1950. She grew up beside the sea in County Dublin. She has worked at boat-building, waitressing and teaching, and lived in England, France, Japan and the United States. She has been active in the women's liberation movement since 1972. In 1974 she was a founder member of Irish Women United, a national feminist group, and also the first lesbian feminist group in Dublin. Worked on *Banshee* and *Wicca,* Irish feminist papers. She has written since childhood and began to write consistently when living in the United States in 1978, where she found women were encouraged to take their interest seriously. 'I write poetry, firstly, because I enjoy it more than any other literary form. But as a feminist writing has a special significance for me. As much as our world is conditioned by words, written and spoken, we women can use words to change reality. The written word was my first introduction to feminism: *Sexual Politics* by Kate Millett, and *The Second Sex* by Simone de Beauvoir. I believe the most important change in women's lives, after economic change, is the development of our own culture. We have been the mirror of men's eyes for centuries. We must remake ourselves in our own image and to do this we must rewrite philosophy, history and theology, and of course express ourselves through every form of creative work. No small task! However, we are beginning. As an Irish woman, writing is especially important to me, because in spite of the intense political activity of the seventies, almost nothing has been recorded of the experience of the Irish lesbians who have come out in this period.' Mary's work has been published in America, England and Ireland. Her first collection, *Kindling,* appeared in 1982.

MARY COGHILL (91). 'I am a feminist, a worker at Sisterwrite Women's Bookshop in London. Living a semi-enclosed life, I call myself a Beguin (Beguins were lay women living in autonomous religious communities in Medieval Western Europe). I am a member of the London Matriarchy Study Group. . . I love to write. Words are always changing meanings for me, and therefore the course of my life. I am writing a book on matriarchal mysticism with Sheila Redmond. This is the study of the passage of love between women.

We are also translating, from the French, the poetry of the "School of Love" by Hadewijch, Beguin of Antwerp.' Mary's poetry has appeared in *One Foot on the Mountain* (1979) and with Diana Scott in *If Women Want to Speak, What Language Do They Use?* (1977); also in publications of the London Matriarchy Study Group.

CATRIONA STAMP (92). 'I was born in Reading, England, 3 May 1950. After university I worked for a while as a town planner. I have lived communally at Laurieston Hall since 1975 and during the past three winters at People in Common (Co-operative Communities in Scotland and the north of England). I've learnt many skills, the most important of which are joinery, plastering and screen printing, from which I mainly earn money for my contribution to the income of the co-operative groups I live in. I have a fifteen-month-old son, who has been looked after communally since birth. I started writing with teenage love poetry and by keeping an erratic diary which covers my first years at Laurieston Hall. The impetus to write something less intensely personal, which could be shared more easily, came from Women's Weeks held at Laurieston, in which small groups of writers would often come together. I also see sharing my writing as an important part of living communally as I want to help create our own culture. Although my son has cut down the time available for writing, he has increased my productivity since I am now far more disciplined. At the moment I prefer to write short stories and articles, some of which have appeared in Laurieston's newsletter and *Communes Network* and I have a project to rewrite and perform mummer's plays.'

FRAN WINANT (93) (106). Fran Winant lives in New York and has been the editor and publisher of Violet Press, a feminist poetry press since 1971. She is the author of *Looking at Women, Dyke Jacket,* and *Goddess of Lesbian Dreams* (1971, 1976, 1980). Her poetry has been used in feminist and gay studies courses at a number of American universities and colleges, and has appeared in a number of key radical and feminist anthologies, notably, *We Become New* and *Mountain Moving Day*. It has also appeared in many American poetry and feminist magazines and she has given many readings in the New York area. She is a member of the Poetry Society of America and Women in the Arts. She is listed in the *Directory of American Poets, Who's Who of American Women* and elsewhere.

DIANA SCOTT (94) (129) (131). I was born in the United States in 1947 and was brought to Europe as a small child. My family on both sides consists very largely of migrants of different sorts going back at least three generations, and a constant theme in my life has been the need to search for the roots of things and to open a space for communication between people of differing views and between people and the worlds they inhabit. In becoming a writer and a seeker after truth I carry on, in a sense, a family tradition; members of my family have been and are now religious believers, ministers, humanists, educators, and writers and journalists of real accomplishment. But I seek to carry on and in a sense redefine this tradition in the light of my position as a feminist scholar and author and the experience of my own integrity as a human being. I am deeply grateful to the many writers who supported me directly and indirectly in making this poetry collection possible, and to the insights of the women's liberation movement without which such books as these don't happen. I earn most of my living by teaching English to Indian, Pakistani and Vietnamese adult students living in Leeds and Bradford. My hobby is road-running: London, 1982, was my first marathon. The three poems above were written in 1975 and 1976 but record experiences that are outside time. This book is, of course, my current gift.

ASPHODEL (95) (127) (132). 'I was born in London in 1921, grew up in the slump, left school at sixteen and believed my aim was to earn a room of my own and £500 a year. Having spent nearly a lifetime doing this I found I'd forgotten what Virginia Woolf had said the project was for. But I spent a long time being a journalist and a single mother, also spending time in left-wing politics, trying always to be independent and never to let myself down as a woman, but only now I am finding out who I am. I had written poetry throughout my life and always lost it; but recently I've had enough confidence and support from other women to stop losing poems! "Asphodel" are the flowers that grow in the Elysian Fields, and I became Asphodel, after nearly a lifetime as Pauline Long, when I came to terms with my own mortality – I found in the concept of the phases of the moon, which are also in every woman, the certainty that the new moon rises after the dark, and will do so, even if one day not for me. I find the women's liberation movement has blessed me and I'm proud I have lived in a time when women at last are able to speak out. I hope more and more will do so.' Of Asphodel's feminist work, articles and poems have appeared in *One Foot on the Mountain* (1979), *Spare Rib, Goddess Shrew, The Politics of Matriarchy, Menstrual Taboos, Women's International Quarterly, Women Speaking* and *London Women's Liberation Newsletter.*

JUDITH KAZANTZIS (96) (113) (124) (133). Judith Kazantzis has had two collections of poetry published: *Minefield* (1977) and *The Wicked Queen* (1980). She has had poetry published in magazines and anthologies and has given readings in places such as the Poetry Society, the I.C.A. and the Oxford Poetry Festival. Recently she has completed a children's novel and has written the introduction to Virago's anthology of women's verse of the First World War, *Scars Upon My Heart.* She reviews poetry for *Spare Rib* and currently runs creative writing classes. Previous publications: *The Gordon Riots* and *Women in Revolt.* 'I have written poetry since I was seven, my first work being one of Spenserian stature (in a school exercise book) entitled *Fairyland.* This book was lost by my mother. I have been interested in reassembling good and bad in women ever since.' Judith Kazantzis was born in 1940 in Oxford and lives in London with her husband and her two children. She says she is an artist on the side.

ASTRA (97) (123). Astra was born on 30 November 1927 in New York City. 'My dad named me for that starry night!' Educated at the High School of Music and Art in Upper Manhattan and taking her B.A. in early childhood education at Queens College, N.Y.C., Astra then taught for twelve years in the New York primary school system, including in two newly built schools in Harlem. Over the past nine years in London she's done paid work in a variety of council and alternative nurseries, including eighteen months as a child-worker at Islington Women's Aid. She writes of this in *Battle Cries* (1981). Though Astra traces her life as a writer back to at least 1959, she says free self-expression only came when she was a member of the Women's Literature Collective between 1972 and 1978. 'I wrote and wrote and wrote; more than forty years of suppressed rage, etc. etc. poured out unceasingly. It was as if entry into the women's liberation movement, mid-1971, had given me permission, outlet and audience for the creative urges I'd tried releasing a decade or more before. At present, I'm in a feminist writers' group where I'm the only poet and currently the least productive member. I'm also part of a feminist poetry group – with one other woman. She's been talking of starting up a feminist press, specifically for poetry. The few feminist presses in the U.K. at this time don't encourage poetry publication enough, despite the fact that more women, feminists and otherwise, write poetry than any other form, I suspect. Writing is my life, or a good portion of it. It's a major means of being politically effective as I want to be.' Astra has been published in many feminist books and magazines.

LESLEY SAUNDERS (98). 'I have reached, more or less what I consider the mid-point in my life, chronologically and emotionally. I wrote poems when I was little, of course, but school quickly put a stop to that. When I started writing again, I took as my mentors poets like Eliot, Hopkins and Lawrence and worked, rather uncomfortably, within the limitations of the disaffected male convention. It wasn't until I bore my children (Leon and Laura, in 1978 and 1981) that feminist traditions and novelties really helped me to make sense of the world (inner and outer) expressively. The meshing of "political" and "personal" events and feelings preoccupies me – I don't yet feel I have the balance right between propaganda and individualism. Poets like Marge Piercy and Pablo Neruda now indicate for me a direction to go in. This year, 1982, most of my writing is centred around drawing together the correspondence, poems, pictures which are the manifestations of a relationship between me and another person into a coherent "political" work.' Published work (in book form) appears in *One Foot on the Mountain* (1979) and *Why Children?* (1980).

STEF PIXNER (110). Stef Pixner was born in London in 1945. She has worked as an artists' model, lecturer in psychology and sociology and women's studies, gardener, feminist therapist and waitress. She was in Hackney Music Workshop; she now writes and performs songs as well as poems. She is currently writing a novel. She is also an artist and often illustrates her poems with her own distinctive drawings. She lives in Hackney in east London and sends reviews and fiction to *Spare Rib.* A more representative selection of her work can be found in *Smile Smile Smile Smile* (1980). Other published work appears in *Licking the Bed Clean* (1978), *One Foot on the Mountain* (1979), and *Hard Feelings* (1979).

ALISON FELL (112). Alison Fell was born in Dumfries, Scotland, in 1944. She trained as a sculptor. She says she became involved with the women's liberation movement in 1969–70 while in Leeds as an art college faculty wife. While in Leeds she had participated in Welfare State, a radical theatre company, and it was as a result of her feminist commitment that she left Leeds for London with the intention of being a member of a women's street theatre group. Initially a member of the Women's Theatre Group, when the group re-formed into two sections, one mounting more 'conventional' stage plays, and the breakaway group undertaking street theatre and other 'actions', Alison found herself in the latter group. It was this involvement that led to the start of her involvement with journalism. The Street Theatre Group mounted a show at the Festival of Light in 1971 – a show shockingly anti-religious and anti-family. The players were instantly arrested. It was Alison Fell's press-release, circulated round the radical and underground journals, that led to an invitation to write for *Ink.* Subsequently she worked for *Red Rag* and *Islington Gutter Press,* and has contributed articles to *Spare Rib* (whose collective editorial board she joined in 1975), *Time Out* and *Oz*. She has held posts as writer-in-residence at several London schools, and in 1980 completed a post-graduate certificate of education at London University. Alison lives with her fourteen-year-old son in their council flat in Newington Green, London, on what she believes may be the very site of Mary Wollstonecraft's pioneering school for girls. Publications include: *Cutlasses and Earrings* (1977), *Licking the Bed Clean* (1978), *One Foot on the Mountain* (1979), *Hard Feelings* (1979), *The Grey Dancer* (1981) and *Smile Smile Smile Smile* (1980).

CHRISTINA JENKINS (114). Christina Jenkins was born in Hackney, London, in the summer of 1962. 'I am an only child, working class, and a feminist. I wrote "Sunday Morning" when I was sixteen; it was my third poem. A week before it was written I had found Sylvia Plath's *Ariel* in the local library. It was the first time I had read poetry written by a woman; before then I had only known poems in men's voices and they had nothing to do with me – and so I hadn't even considered writing poetry before. After reading Plath there was no stopping me! I'm now living in Brighton because I'm at Sussex University (doing literature) but I'm looking forward to getting back to London. I haven't worked on very many poems since university (university has nothing to do with personal creativity!) but I'm planning to get going again once I leave. I look forward to that. Poetry is my right arm!'

JO BARNES (115). 'Clinic Day' is taken from Jo Barnes's memorable autobiographical booklet *Arthur and Me*. Jo says: 'I am pleased that "Clinic Day" is going to be in your anthology. Just as I was beginning to lose faith in my ability to write even a recipe. I was born on 26 April 1941 in Bristol of working-class parents. My father worked in an engineering factory and later on the docks. Primary school was followed by secondary school, where I was an unremarkable pupil. I left school at the age of fifteen in 1956. From school I trained in data processing, which cast me in this deadly mould for many years. I managed to break out and for five years I worked in a hospital at various clerical duties. I was married in 1968 and I have two children, a daughter born in 1970 and a son born in 1972 and we live in Keynsham, a semi-rural area between Bristol and Bath. My writing is drawn from my own experiences and those of my family. I began writing around 1973 when my children were small and I was largely confined to domestic boredom and needing a creative outlet. For the last four years I have worked from home, doing a not very adequate job of book-keeping for my husband and continuing to write spasmodically. *Arthur and Me* was published in 1979.'

PAT ARROWSMITH (117) (122). Pat Arrowsmith, pacifist and socialist, has been editorial assistant at Amnesty International, London, since 1971. She was educated at Cheltenham Ladies College and Newnham College, Cambridge, among others and she has held many community and manual jobs. She committed herself to the anti-nuclear movement from the very earliest days of the Campaign for Nuclear Disarmament in this country; she has been gaoled ten times as a prisoner of conscience on various anti-war issues; and has contested a number of parliamentary seats on various peace issues. She is a member of War Resisters International, Troops Out Movement, British Withdrawal from Northern Ireland Campaign; the Campaign for Nuclear Disarmament and the Anti-Nazi League. Recent publications include *Breakout* (poems and drawings from prison) (1975), *On the Brink* (1981) and a novel, *The Prisoner* (1982), about a day in the life of a disabled bed-ridden woman. Pat Arrowsmith says: 'The first and great commandment is: Try to practise what you preach,' and her lifelong political and pacifist commitment shows to what a notable extent she has kept to this.

GILLIAN E. HANSCOMBE (119). Gillian Eve Hanscombe was born in Melbourne, Australia, where she read English at Melbourne and Monash Universities. Since coming to live in London in 1969 she has worked variously at teaching, office work, journalism and selling. She graduated D.Phil. from St Hughs College, Oxford, in 1979 after writing a thesis on the English feminist novelist, Dorothy Richardson. Apart from articles and poems published in journals, she is co-author with Jackie Forster of *Rocking the Cradle: Lesbian Mothers – A Challenge in Family Living,* also *Art of Life: Dorothy Richardson and the Rise of Feminist Consciousness* and *Between Friends* – the last two published in 1982. *Hecate's Charms,* a cycle of poems, was published in Australia in 1976. At present she is working as a news reporter for *Gay News.*

JANET DUBÉ (120) (121). 'I was born in Fulham, London, during the Second World War. I began writing in 1968 in, and after some years out of, an undiagnosed state of post-natal depression. My work has appeared in *It'll Take a Long Time,* (1977) and *One Foot on the Mountain* (1979). See also *Meditation for Our Children* and *Housewives' Choice* (1982).

DESIRÉE FLYNN (125) (128). Desirée Flynn was born Sheila Desirée Savory Rodd, on 30 April 1917 at Hampstead Heath, London, the only daughter of an American mother of Austrian descent and an Australian father of English descent. She is a sixth generation Australian. Until the age of six she travelled with her father in

Europe, subsequently settling with him in Sydney. She wrote poems throughout her childhood, won prizes at school and often read out poems to her father's friends. As an adult she worked and travelled and married Roderic Flynn. They had two daughters and one son – the children in 'From the Rain Forest'. Desirée Flynn continued working and writing poems whenever possible. A collection of poems was privately published to commemorate her sixtieth birthday. She now lives outside Sydney, participates in literary groups and keeps on writing. Of the two poems collected here, 'From the Rain Forest' won second place in the Henry Lawson Australian and New Zealand Poetry Competition in 1975 and 'The Collector' was highly commended in the same competition in 1976.

NAOMI REPLANSKY (126) (130). Naomi Replansky was born in New York City and has been writing poetry since the age of ten. *Ring Song,* her first collection of poems, was published in 1952. Her second book, *I Met My Solitude,* is still unpublished. Her work has been reprinted widely in anthologies; translations of her poems have been published in France and Germany. She has also translated poetry from the French, German and Yiddish; a version by her of Brecht's *Saint Joan of the Stockyards* was produced in New York in 1978. She has earned her living at a variety of factory, office and technical jobs. In 1981 she was poet-in-residence at Pitzer College in California. She now works as a computer programmer.

LORNA MITCHELL (135). Lorna Mitchell is a member of Stramullion Co-operative Ltd, a Scottish-based feminist publishing collective. Articles of hers have appeared in *Spare Rib, Outcome* and *Scottish Women's Liberation Journal;* also in *One Foot on the Mountain* (1979) and *Hens in the Hay* (1980). She has completed a science fiction novel *120 Light Years From Babylon,* as yet unpublished.

STEPHANIE MARKMAN (136). Stephanie Markman is a member of Stramullion Co-operative. The full illustrated version of 'The Rime of the Ancient Feminist' was first published in autumn 1981. Stephanie Markman was born in Edinburgh in 1952, lives in Edinburgh and is currently studying linguistics at Edinburgh University. She has had work published in the *Leveller* and *Spare Rib* and *One Foot on the Mountain* (1979); she co-authored *Hens in the Hay* (1980), and a short story about life after the Bomb, 'Down Under in the Nuclear Family', was published in pamphlet form. She is currently working on a radio play about domestic violence.

ANON. AND OTHERS. Anna Adams (see (53) and (54)), writing in December 1981 in the *Guardian* of women's tendency to remain anonymous, tells of a woman architect who collaborated anonymously with her husband for many years – the projects, the books of which she had written so many chapters appeared under his name. When the marriage collapsed she was left with no independent reputation of her own. 'Then she realised that it had been immoral of her not to have signed her own work. It may have been good work and to do it without acknowledgement was altruistic, selfless, and for the general benefit of humanity – except for herself. And she had a right to share in the general good . . . Truthfulness and justice demanded her signature.'

'Poem for Jacqueline Hill' (138) was written in the week following the murder of the Leeds student on 17 November 1980. Funded by donations, the poem was printed in many thousands and distributed free through the radical distribution networks to bookshops, women's centres and other community centres in the U.K. Extracts appeared in a number of newspapers and magazines, and the poem was quoted in 'instant books' completed after Peter Sutcliffe's trial. The purpose of the poem was to communicate that the 'Ripper', was one of many men making violent attacks on women, and the fear that women experienced at the time of this murder was no isolated event but a fear that to a lesser or greater degree was a constant part of their lives. The leaflet in which the poem appeared carried a mention of the nationwide feminist Women against Violence against Women campaign (which may still be contacted c/o Women's Place, 48 William IV Street, London WC2), and encouraged readers of the poem to support it, or similar groups concerned with the issue of violence against women.

Woven into the text of the poem is a substantial quantity of data taken from newspaper, television and radio reports, feminist actions, and the thoughts and feelings women and men expressed at the time. Because the writer wished to interpose her own self as little as possible between her readers and these ghastly events that were being experienced with equal intensity by thousands and because of the responsibility she experienced towards all those who were working towards a world in which such murders did not happen, she remained anonymous. All these considerations to some extent still apply; but so does the argument that women should honour and acknowledge their own work. So I will. I wrote it.

Also on the subject of anonymity and acknowledgement, I'd like to record my regret that biographical details of the authors of the poems taken from *Shush, Mum's Writing* (1978), Maureen Burge, (116, 118), and *Houseplant* (1977), Rosemary Norman, (101, 102), Felicity Napier (108), Susan Wallbank (109) and Jennifer Armitage (87), were not obtainable at the time of going to press. We'd like to hear from them so their particulars may be included in any possible future editions and any enquirers may be put in touch with them meanwhile.

Valerie Sinason

THE RENAMING (86)

It began in her pram
when she named the blue-plate sky
and the bird-faces that flocked
to feast

And that gave her time
                    to grow
wrappings of words, ribbons of words,

And the pram ticked like a parcel bomb
but only her mouth
endlessly exploding . . .

And they smiled so sweetly
as they ate her dolls and bears
she knew no toy could hold her

and gazing higher
she named rooves and chimneys
but they followed
eyes in her eyes
mouths in her mouth

and they ransacked her streets and cities
trees and sunlight and leaves

and straining to keep awake at night
and make the darkness her own
she named the moon and stars
and called the night sea
          the night sea
to help
      let her be
            still

And the night sea rose
in the fourth corner of her cot
and they could not swallow it.

She tried to rest in the nightmare pause
between waves
but there were no names to hide her,
there was nothing left to name

and the bird-faces were coming blurred and wavy
through the blind waters.

And cold and dry-eyed in her cot
(her tears long-since named away)
she began again

and named the sky
plate.

Jennifer Armitage

(87) TO OUR DAUGHTER

And she is beautiful, our daughter.
Only six months, but a person.
She turns to look at everything, out walking.
All so precious. I mustn't disturb it with words.
People are like great clowns,
Blossom like balloons, black pigeons like eagles,
Water beyond belief.

She holds out her hand to air,
Sea, sky, wind, sun, movement, stillness,
And wants to hold them all.
My finger is her earth connection, me, and earth.

Her head is like an apple, or an egg.
Skin stretched fine over a strong casing,
Her whole being developing from within
And from without: the answer.

And she sings, long notes from the belly or the throat,
Her legs kick her feet up to her nose,
She rests – laid still like a large rose.

She is our child,
The world is not hers, she has to win it.

Michele Roberts

THE SIBYL'S SONG (88)

having hooded my face with hair
having hung, all night long
lips apart, over a silent pit
having crouched, having borne down
and down, having yelled
having delivered myself
having danced, having bitten
cloth, beaten air
until the song came
having delivered myself of a strong song
I collapse, laughing, with dissolved bones

she who came to me, she who called out loud
she who licked at my ear
like flame, and sank in
deep as a wound, she who swelled in me
she whose winged breath
wrestles with mud and
shapes it to pots and houses
she is my lady, she is the secret word

having lain with many men
having remained virgin, unmarried
having loved women, having shown
forth my proud belly, my songs
– I shall burn for this

I will sing high in the fire
my body her torch: oh let
the fierce goddess
come

Harriet Rose

(89) THE SUCCUBUS

Cased in your bone and plaster
you stare where the land stretches
like eyeless sockets
out.

'The divil's coming out yonder'
screamed the old man
hearing you sing, seeing your trousers
rolled up to your knees
(and the flesh is evil).
And a man with a ram's horn
blew a note through the trees.
And the old man said
'the devil the devil is coming'
And he sent his children hiding.

And the ram's horn went cold
like a note from the sounding streams
of the shadowless heavens.

Asking my name
while the seas blew through the ram's horn
and the orange light streamed through the sounds
asking my name, your voice stopped.
I have no name, no name.
I have no papers.

I have stood on the cliffs
with my thoughts without word
with the lines of the light
windstrokes that hammer
the air's wavering ridges with movement.
And you came from behind
and then saw that your hands
were clasped tight round my shoulders.
And a wingspread of cloud

rode bareback on the funnels of flame
and we stared at the sky.

But you went where the old man went
yelling 'Father, Father'
searching through the sunlight for your father
who is blind except to darknesses.
And I run.
I don't care if the rocks cut my feet.
I am afraid of the name that you will name me.

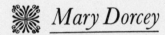

Mary Dorcey

SEA FLOWER (90)

Your thighs your belly;
their sweep and strength,
your breasts so sudden
nipples budding in my hands.
The sheen of your back
under my palms,
your flanks smooth as flame.

Your skin – that inner skin
like silk,
your mouth deepening
full as an orchid,
honey on my tongue.

The dizzy lurch and sway;
sea flowers under water,
changing skins with every touch
and then and again, that voice
– your voice, breaking over me,
opening earth with its call
and rocking the moon in her tide.

Mary Coghill

(91) KNOWING

I dug in with all the spirit of spring
delightfully teased by the sweet scent
of the fresh turned soil – earth meets sun
for the first time – darkness to warmth and light.
Let lie and sleep for the frost to work
and snow and rain and in due time
plough, fold in, nurturance of secrecy:
I have the seeds, given over and over
stored and harboured, grains of now and ever
planted and I catch my breath, I let
the west wind welcome first and breathe
only after as memory of beckoner.

You grew, I grew, bathed in sun, balmed
by warmth, hallowed round in rain and my
thoughts echo and cradle the harmony:
all this I cannot change and watch,
in the heat and the waiting, turn,
we all turn and see that the moon harbours
all that we ever need to know:
we all have a harvest to reap –
I have sharpened and refined
caressed the waiting over, and now
I cut all growth and stem and yield
the fruit, or head, or heart, or ears
and I listen: oh sister – where is
the granary? I am a winnow sieve and
without you all the grains will fall through.

Catriona Stamp

REBIRTH (92)

Water flooded everywhere
dripping over the edges of the plate of the world.
Spring stream rushing, impetuous white hurly-burly.
Slow-winding, green-pooled, golden-leaved in autumn.
Cart-track, thick mud carved by wheels,
black bowls laced with ice, glistening in the winter light.

Those floods washed me to the sea,
where waves dragged at my peripheries,
tentacled to my skin,
ebbing me away to be dissolved
and respun in the whirlpools of time.

I was laid bare to the bone of my spool.
I was harrowed –
the tines of the harrow drawn through my flesh;
the red blood pulsing,
repulsing,
the slivers of flesh sliced from the bone.
I was stripped and left naked.

I hung upside down in the womb
a second time,
hearing the thunder and surge
of water-distorted, body-absorbed voices
boom
beyond comprehension.

I longed for birth,
stretched out for understanding,
pushed through the new-found opening
at the base of the womb,
and fell, warm and confident
with many others through black space;
no limits known,
and filled with pleasure.

No longer gravity bound
by womb or air or sea,
we fell gracefully,
with poise,
like dancers,
full of faith,
bodies growing like wings,
unfolding like flowers.

The sky of our falling was velvet –
smooth skin of a black woman,
spangled with sweat drops of light
falling faster and brighter toward us,
spinning,
as we spun on our spindles,
balls of thread growing
from the creative void –
woven for eternity.

Fran Winant

(93) A SACRED GROVE

What would it be like
for the landscape of the moon
no longer to be your place,
for you to wander green earth,
claiming it as home,
for you not to smile
with thin-lipped welcome
at despair,
calling it a privilege,
equating it with love,
for you to bury
the bones of your hunger,
gnawed rough these years,

wearing your teeth down
while keeping them white,
for you to remove
the Abandon All Hope sign
you found it amusing to keep
over your door,
for you to step into open sunlight,
not always feeling it stark
as a bare bulb in a hall,
for you to plant
a stand of trees
in your interior,
a sacred grove
that swayed and sang
when the wind passed through.

Diana Scott

LUCY TAKING BIRTH (94)

Lucy goes down the celestial escalator in light
sees falling stars rushing up and outwards
Lucy, a new Lucifer or Nautilus will penetrate the heart of
darkness
Do not fear the bottom she says to the scurrying stars or
fishes
I know it, it is for me they are waiting

Lucy, an unholy Alice,
descends the precipice behind her shut eyelids
Lucy is not frightened: What frightens Lucy?
She is the Creatrix of the sea-bed light
the twisty weeds, the dear pulpy squids are hers
She knows what spangly and fearful construction
beckons from the bottom

Lucy goes down the celestial escalator in light
sees falling stars rushing up and outwards
Lucy, a new Lucifer or Nautilus will penetrate the heart
   and darkness
Do not fear the bottom she says to the scurrying stars or
   fishes
I know it

Lucy, a returned diver lies breathing for real
in the precious dawn
The sun climbs in a white cuphandle arc
over the pale day
Lucy has survived this night
And has one created days hard grace

Asphodel

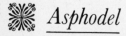

(95) FULL MOON IN MALTA

She brought us a month noisy with rain
As she swung her shining boat over the sky
Loosing cool winds, unaccustomed clouds
Mirrored in black water, heavy with seaweed.
She thrust seaspray high against the rocks
Drenching the chance-comer.

As she gained the top of the sky
She burst into a globe fruit
And day changed to sunlight timorously
In a patchwork of mud and moss and winking petals.

Would the Spring fail this year? Had she moved below
Indignant at last, of our use of her? Sounding an inexorable
Anathema on human despoilers?

Would the spring sit underground this year?
Forever?

As I walked down the grey road in the afternoon dusk
Seeing a patchy field, where wild daisies danced in
                    thorns and stones
And a group of goats backed down to harbour;
In the green folds of the thin grass
Suddenly, another fruit, another boat, another pattern,
Suddenly whole groups, among the grass and the thistles
                    and the wild clover
Suddenly in the singing evening, as the first star climbed
  upwards
Suddenly in the dusty road, bending mildly towards me
In the damp evening, Suddenly I saw, looked again and saw
The merciful corn.

Judith Kazantzis

ARACHNE (96)

After years of relative clumsiness
she found her fingers, ten shuttles
keying one, the actual:
thinking and throwing, throwing and thinking,
the enclosed room,
the working stool;
growing quite old, her hair silver
in untidy hanks, according to everyone else.
But she brushed aside their meals
and used the trays to weight down the sections.

One day, without a warning tremor
the cloth danced.
Her fingers assuaged the silk thread with flame
and began something
that curled over the floor like the folds
of the Python.

She realised she had her prophecies
at fingertip length; and never stopped
for love or lunch:
the rough thrown wood shaft, familiar to touch,
the rows of opening eyes
kohl fringed, colour of filled crater or sky
shining, caustic, gazing
sunk back into the skull
and from there, informative.

Her hands were filament.
She finished eyes as large as saucers or millstones.

The hands rise to the mouth,
running the lips, as tired as dogs:
the soft mouth of concluding
for the ceding hands.
Then at fingerlength roars the goddess again,
the wrong one,
out of touch with reading cards, sight, phases
flames, chances and what have you
but powerfully having the power of changes
like other quick minds, toughened up.
It seems she dislikes restfulness,
the retirement of hands to soft refuges,
crescent nurse of lips after the
incessant hard shuttle.

Arachne stuck on the beam.
Her knowledge shrank to what it had been.
With one thread to drop,
coil up, coil round,
she tries, stolid, millions of goes,
gets to a limited yard,
makes dust.
The rarity, the odd go, the oddity,
the flaming cloth.

Astra

DAUGHTERS (97)

i dedicate this poem
to my unborn daughters
the ones i always wanted
and never had
as i yearned for sisters
when i was little
and when i was big

(fourteen years ago
the doctor congratulated me
on producing two sons
within three years –
the operative word being
'sons')

to my unborn daughters
i wish you
        strength in locating/confronting
        the core of yourself
        tenacity in retaining it
        arrogance in nurturing it
        conviction that it/you are whole
        a vision of feminism's future
        a network of women friends/lovers and
        a very long life to make all of this happen

during this lifetime of mine
perhaps i shall give birth to myself
so i too can achieve what i wish for you
                                        my daughters

in my next life
we shall meet
            and love each other

Lesley Saunders

(98) MOTHERS OF SONS

For Halima

I had wanted a daughter.
You bore the son you hoped for
Exactly seven weeks later.

And here we are
Wheeling them side by side
Through the park and communing
Under the high empty blue
Of a February sky
As if this were the scene
That the past had all along intended

And the score of generous years
From our first school days together until now
Had helter-skelter and without a word to us
Gone and squashed themselves, smack, into pictures
In a diorama! The limelight shifts; we take turns
Peering over each other's shoulder,
Shaking our heads and laughing, gripped about the heart
By these animations we cannot halt or alter.
We replay the best tableaux, speak our parts spiritedly,
Counting off the episodes like rosary beads
(And then, yes and then, do you remember . . .)
As if we could amend this passing of time
Or fend it away.
(We need this: we need more than this,
To give ourselves back our precious pasts
Though the gift feels known a thousandfold.)

Still, some things won't stay inside this magic space,
Will not yet be lit up and faded at will,
Most of all our births and deaths –
You alone have made the unpardonable acquaintance,
As you stepped into the shadow of those dear deaths
I could be only an onlooker.

Well, and then, and then –
A season or so ago
Leaving neither of us unscathed, unwrung,
Came the blood and griping
And I and you gave birth

And here we are, figures in the scene.

* * *

Our sons, our sons!
Ha! we have brought forth and multiplied ourselves.
Out of nothing, nothing comes, the saying is:
We know the stunning news, that out of nothing
Quite brazenly they come, womb-fruit,
And dwell wonderful among us.

Now we are mothers, now we have sons.
What does it mean? Have you, have I, ever thought,
Hugging these scraps to our breasts?
Our sons, the heirs to our ways:
The first-born, the god-given,
Leaders of men, pioneers, begetters of dynasties,
Philosophers, architects of empire, poets and lovers,
– Also slave-owners, murderers, wifebeaters and rapers,
Boot boys, jeerers and jokers, warmongers, oppressors
Official of home and state, greedy despoilers
Of our bodies and souls.
And we, their angels of mercy, their sweet earth,
Martyrs that they shall spring into glory,
Good, wise, gentle Mother
– Also the witch with knife in hand and teeth bared,
Killing and devouring, smothering and deserting . . .

These are not myth.

I know them, have lived them these last months,
Inhabited heaven and hell and everywhere between –
Tell me, haven't you?

O where can we find rest among all these weary mirages,
Where can we feel safe from these huge totems
Whose carved truculent faces always block the sky?
Our sons, the heirs to our estate.
How can we make it not so?
Each babe's patrimony, a mansion or a millstone
Flung into its cradle, accrues from generation
Unto generation, until someone can cry
Stop! The parental ghosts hunt on relentless,
Demanding either rest or else redemption
From deeds they have failed to do,
Acts they have not owned, love they have not had
Or bestowed – the needs they ignore take flesh
In the children, dance in the marrow
Of their bones to cripple them in turn,
To be solved or suffered again.
Life makes no allowances. This knife-edge
Precious time, these all or nothing years
Are where my past lives on
And his future casts its shadow.
Unless I keep my hoard of relics to myself,
Say Hallo to the outrageous ghosts, cry
Stop! my son will be the wearer
Of my life's mark, grow up grieving
That his life is not his own, grow old
Trailing the foot that could not leave
His mother's womb.

(What heritage awaits his coming of age?
Will he remember me, will he want to,
In my old age? How will he remember me
In his old age, his mother and his endower?
As the bundle forever clamped
Upon his neck, sucking the life juice from his heart –
I go on wondering, and yes,
I fear it will be so.)

His cries unsettle me,
His father's father's in his stubborn jaw,
And in his smile I see my mother's face
And in his woe;
His gaze reveals quite other worlds, his laughing
Looses me, his wails send coursing through me
Love and hate and all things I fear.

Out of the mouths . . .

Out of the mouths of sons
Come mothers, creeping,
Dancing.

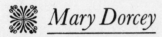

Mary Dorcey

FIRST LOVE

You were tall and beautiful.
You wore your long brown hair
wound about your head,
your neck stood clear and full
as the stem of a vase.
You held my hand in yours
and we walked slowly, talking
of small familiar happenings
and of the lost secrets of
your childhood. It seems it was

Always autumn then.
The amber trees shook. We laughed
in a wind that cracked the leaves
from black boughs and set them scuffling
about our feet, for me to trample still
and kick in orange clouds
about your face. We would climb dizzy
to the cliff's edge and stare down
at a green and purple sea, the

Wind howling in our ears, as it
tore the breath from white cheeked waves.
You steadied me against
the wheeling screech of gulls, and i
loved to think that but for your strength
i would tumble to the rocks below
to the fated death, your stories made me
dream of. I don't remember
that i looked in your eyes or that we
ever asked an open question. Our thoughts

Passed through our blood, it seemed,
and the slightest pressure of our hands
decided all issues wordlessly.
We watched in silence by the shore
the cold spray against our skin,
in mutual need of the water's fierce,
inhuman company, that gave promise
of some future, timeless refuge from
all the fixed anxieties of our world.
As we made for home

We faced into the wind, my thighs
were grazed by its icy teeth, you
gathered your coat about me and i
hurried our steps towards home, fire
and the comfort of your sweet, strong tea.
We moved bound in step.
You sang me songs of Ireland's sorrows
and of proud women, loved and lost.
I knew then, they set for me
a brilliant stage of characters, who

Even now, can seem more real
than my most intimate friends.
We walked together, hand in hand.
You were tall and beautiful,
you wore your long brown hair wound

about your head, your neck stood
clear and full as the stem of a vase.
I was young – you were my mother
and it seems, it was always
autumn then.

Michele Roberts

MAGNIFICAT (100)

(for Sian, after thirteen years)

oh this man
what a meal he made of me
how he chewed and gobbled and sucked
in the end he spat me all out

you arrived on the dot, in the nick
of time, with your red curls flying
I was about to slip down the sink like grease
I nearly collapsed, I almost
wiped myself out like a stain
I called for you, and you came, you voyaged
fierce as a small archangel with swords and breasts
you declared the birth of a new life
in my kitchen there was an annunciation
and I was still, awed by your hair's glory

you commanded me to sing of my redemption

oh my friend, how
you were mother for me, and how
I could let myself lean on you
comfortable as an old cloth
familiar as enamel saucepans
I was a child again, pyjama'ed
in winceyette, my hair plaited, and you

listened, you soothed me like cake and milk
you listened to me for three days, and I poured
it out, I flowed all over you like wine, like oil
you touched the place where it hurt
at night, we slept together in my big bed
your shoulder eased me towards dreams

when we met, I tell you
it was a birthday party, a funeral
it was a holy communion
between women, a Visitation
it was two old she-goats butting
and nuzzling each other in the smelly fold

Rosemary Norman

(101) MY SON AND I

My son wears a nappy
And waterproof pants
He shits and he pisses
Whenever he wants.

He has no intentions
Not evil or good
But his tears have a function
To get him his food.

For love of the world
I have taken control
Of the self-centred workings
Of bladder and bowel.

That is less than enough
As too plainly appears,
But my will runs to waste
In incontinent tears.

CABBAGE (102)

Brassica (oleracea) is a cabbage
She is cruciferous, that is
Bears with patience
Four equal petals to every flower.

Only the terminal leaf-bud is active
Forming a head.
She is her head, cabbage
From Latin 'caput'

Brassica, though, is what
The Romans call her, along with
Kale (acephala), sprouts (gemmifera)
And all their kin.

Kale (headless), sprouts (many headed)
Cabbage contained.
She gestures inward, inward,
The cabbage (vegetable).

Astra

NOW OR NEVER (103)

seven years ago
at forty-five
i knew it was time
for a rockbottom change
time to kick over my traces
time to stand my life on its head
time to sow my autonomous oats
time to put my money where my mouth was
because i couldn't bear not to
any longer

which is not to say
it happened in one night
or even in one year
by magic and by spells
aided by rational and sympathetic talk
with my family
(quite the contrary)
that it was trauma free
that i didn't have
insomnia   backache   guilt   anxiety   frantic fears
savage rages   homicidal scenes   suicidal sobbings
that for a long time i didn't become
someone unrecognisable
to myself

but it was literally
                    change or die
because of my being middle aged
not despite it
because of knowing in my gut
time was jogging onwards
and i deserved something
                              better
                                    for myself
                                                now
or never

Valerie Sinason

(104) WILL YOU COME OUT NOW?

Will the lady with locker key 43
please come out of the water.

There is a baby crying in her locker.

It is beginning to upset the potted plants
the poolside carpet arches its green spine
smoke drifts from the solarium
and the steam from the showers makes it hard
to see to hear
in this luxurious complex.

Will you come out now?

In the peace
at the centre of the world
you are turning slowly
in the clear waters

A cry breaks into ripples
too many to be heard
so many moving colours,
so many bright circles . . .

Will the lady . . . lady . . .

Sweet rockabye baby
my lockerbye baby
cries breaking in the airless square.

She has eaten the sticky silence
the voice that did not return
buttercup arms and smell of warm bread.

She drinks back
a procession of tears
a necklace of rippling shadows
A swimming pool shines
in the corner of each eye.
She blinks it back.

Behind the raw plug of her mouth
a giant tear is forming.

WILL YOU COME OUT NOW?

Michele Roberts

(105) MADWOMAN AT RODMELL

she strolls in the valley, alone
her ears scan the warning
twanging of birds
her boots plop and suck in the mud's grip

the sky is a cold gold spoon
sun tart and sweet
in the cup of hills licked
clean by the gulp of cows
– at the cup's lip, the foam
and crust of milk, a swell of clouds
and yellow plums; leaves curl
like the peel in marmalade

the world is her mouth
a sour swill of yells

trees scar, and suddenly
redden; bright berries of blood and teeth
hang in the hedge; the bad
baby is out; she
bites through the net; she swarms
free, fizzing; she thunders like bees in a box
maddened for honey and her mama

her lips clang shut on mean rations
she swallows the river
and mourns on down, a thin bellyful

Fran Winant

TO BEGIN (106)

to begin
to continue to begin
to begin over
to continue beginning over
to begin and continue beginning
over and over again
not to have the strength to begin
not to know anymore
how to begin
how dare you not have the strength
you won't get anywhere
unless you begin
everyone has to begin somewhere
beginning for ten years
beginning for twenty
learning
forgetting
being told
you have to learn more
doing
undoing
being told to do more
being told to begin
for the joy of it
love your process
always beginning
never worrying about the end
caught in this moment
stunned
fixed
between desire
hope
wonder
a child kneeling

you have only to begin
again

Valerie Sinason

(107) IN THE BEGINNING

The sky was gold in those days
and the earth a table of brown marble
and Eve is sitting cross-legged
quietly waiting for food.

She braids her hair with flowers
and coloured grasses
so as to not know she is hungry.

But I am hungry, she cries,
growing thinner, waiting,
a delicate shadowing of bone.
She wants to go back to the source
of all things
She wants to find where she began.

God the Mother is knitting a
warm winter coat for Snake.
'Don't tell Eve,' She threatens,
flashing Her forked eyes.
'Or else . . .'

(Snake has forgotten what he once remembered.
Snake has forgotten
there was ever anything to remember.
He grows fatter, sleepier,
Snake is forgetting his purpose.)

God the Mother slams down Her knitting
and thunders to Eve
wearing Her dress of trembling animals.

'EAT' She commands, unhingeing Her
ribcage of sky and earth.

Eve looks at Her tombstone teeth
and the rows upon rows of bonewhite shelves
and the food of many colours
that always ended red
that always ended with the quiver
in the heart of the lettuce
and the tiny cry in the spot in the egg
trembling through its shell.

'Let me know something else,' cries Eve.

God the Mother cracks Her shelves down to the bone.
'And the cupboard is bare,' She screams,
opening up the deepfreeze of Her commandments.

'But I want to know deep in my core,' pleads Eve.

'What will happen?' she wonders, sobbing,
running to the basement flat of Snake.
He comforts her with the memory of his forgetting
and then he begins to remember to remember.
'What will happen?' pleads Eve.

Felicity Napier

HOUSEPLANT (108)

You are my stick, my prop
My tendrils cling to you.
I am not neglected;
I am even admired,
Encouraged to climb high,
Climb close to you
So you influence my growth.
My roots are moist,

There is space in my pot
But I stand in a room that faces north –
I never feel the sun
From that spot.
I am denied joy,
No other word will do,
And a reason for putting forth flowers.

Susan Wallbank

(109) WHY SO MANY OF THEM DIE

**YOUR HOUSEPLANT IS A DELICATE THING.
FOLLOW THESE INSTRUCTIONS CAREFULLY
AND IT WILL BRING YOU YEARS OF PLEASURE.**

I am your houseplant; you are my keeper.
You are my succour, I am your creeper.

Pluck me/pot me/peat me/feed me/water me
talk to me/weed me/heat me/seed me/deflower me
prune me/light me/tend me. **HOURLY**

Stef Pixner

(110) A DAY IN THE LIFE . . .

Today I cleared out the kitchen with Dougie so Hedley could sand the kitchen floor.

It was a Saturday today. Sun came through the window squares and lit up the dust.

Today I smoked cigarettes I didn't want to smoke.

I washed up meticulously; plates, bowls, cups, cutlery, pans. I wiped the draining board and emptied the crumbs from the drawers.

Today Dave and I fucked but I didn't want to kiss him because his mouth tastes funny in the morning.

Today I felt nauseous with grey anxiety as we drove to buy a reconditioned vacuum cleaner, Dougie and I. The sky turned grey, too, in the world outside the car.

Today my room was calm as a temple. The cat came in it for the first time for weeks.

Today I pulled my diaphragm out of my vagina. I found a small basin of dark blood.

Today Rachel's face flooded with love. 'I'm jealous,' she said with a mischievous and defiant certainty. I watched her face harden and soften by turns.

Today my fingers itched to play the guitar and I found myself singing a song.

Today I was delighted to find a jar of whole nutmegs; I had thought that we had no nutmegs.

Today my orgasm was frantic and elusive like the pot of gold at the rainbow's end.

Today I gave Lisa a massage, and I liked the feel of her back.

Today pains gripped either side of my neck like oak tree roots or eagle's claws.

Today I wrote a list of complaints. I'll act on them later.

Today with Dougie, I carried out the heavy oak table and the fridge, slippery with years of egg drippings and grease.

Today Dave licked my belly button and I had a funny sensation somewhere far down inside.

Today I lay in a deep green bath with my toes sticking out at the end, between the taps.

Afterwards, I put on a clean white shirt.

Today Gillian introduced me to a group, according to whose information bureaucratic omissions and half truths are converted into hard facts. She works for the group at home.

Today I spilled blood on the bathroom floor. I wiped it up without a trace.

Today Dave bought a Chinese flute although he's stony broke. I said to Rachel: 'I want to destroy his body!' and made a fist.

Today he looked at me with smiling eyes and I withdrew.

Today I crept near him fondly and he turned away.

He laid his head on my breasts and I put my arms round him. Then he went out and I took up my pen.

Today I saw flecks of yellow in his eyes.

Today I noticed my hands gesturing in the air, giving my words a dancing shape.

Today I loved my lover's thighs, and the innocence of his bum.

Today I smelled sawdust and white spirit and dreamed that I gave up art for the sake of flattery.

Michele Roberts

(111) OUT OF CHAOS OUT OF ORDER OUT

behind glass, my room is neat
white paint, books
little boxes, bowls, a hundred
images of women
I am self-contained as tulips

chaos is away from me:
desolation of the heart
lurching in black ribs
of trees, through yards –
a scrap of red balloon
that seeks and flaps
it tears on thorns of silence;
there in the garden are my plants, too
small green tips: a huge
desiring mountain
pushes underground
angry buds that break
through earth, through unexpected
gaps, and out
of dreams; the pear-tree blossoms
like a white cloth, lace-edged, flung
across my mouth to muffle sobs;
the compost-heap: all the year's
leavings, and the next year's
rich dirt and acts

I call them back inside with me
from gardens, load
my arms with them:
the child screaming for a pricked balloon
flourishing her furious handkerchief
the woman who wants, whose heart
lurches, and whose words
begin to green

who is frightened of that
who sits and hugs herself
who stirs the clutter in her little room

Alison Fell

(112) SIGNIFICANT FEVERS

A January night. Moonlight
strikes the window. Six sweaters
heaped on the chair,
two pairs of jeans each
containing crumpled knickers.

Proper little girls don't lose their clothes,
the text in the head goes; they fold them
the night before, they dream of piles
of linen neat as new exercise books.

Hot-head, scaly-skinned,
feeble and feverish,
I toss under the weight of quilts.

Liz rings up miserable,
comes round with lemons and whisky.
Her blouse has an ironed crease
down the outside of each sleeve.

Lévi-Strauss if I understand him right
says that women disrupt the man-made
opposition between nature and culture.

We nod and drink whisky. The
significance of the fever mounts.

There's no word for the feeling women
have of being in the wrong before
they even open their mouths,
Dale Spender says.

Provisional love. Too much of nothing
can make a woman ill-at-ease.
I'm feeling warren,
hollowburnt. I object to this
set-up, let it be said.

The pale princess on her timid
bed never talks back.
She's dying, but
terribly pleased you asked.

Life is short as a shoelace,
but who knows it?
'68,' I say, 'the politics of desire –
will we see it again?'
Liz says she wants everything *now*,
everything on offer.
Both of us agree that what we
would most relish at the moment
is to be madly desired. We feel
in the wrong about this too.

Lonelyhearts, classified:
John, 34, interests publishing, astrology,
walking. Own car, limited income.
Seeks intelligent feminist 20-40,
Box Y288.

I disagree with Liz: No,
they can't all be creeps.
I'm feeling oldmould, grabbitted.

In the West, much was made
of killing dragons. St. George
and the other heroes with all
their hardware, littering
the ley lines with sites
of slaughter and canonisation.

In the structures of fever,
never a dull moment.
(The spiral round the stone,
the spiral deep in the storm.)

In the East they bound
women's feet and believed

in the harmony and man and landscape,
paths of wind, water and dragons,
forces which must not be impeded
by rails, tramways, television aerials.

Sweat stains the sheets. I
have boils, Liz has cold sores:
energies seeking escape routes.

Clean neckties of news announcers,
rescuing us from dragons.
Clean underpants. A consensus.
Under the newsdesk their toes
manipulate electric trainsets.

Proper little girls don't lose their clothes,
the text in the dream goes.
I'm feeling ragbitter,
hellworthy.

The nuclear train which is found
on no timetable sidles
through London in the night,
containing dead hearts blazing:
an energy which has been eaten
and will eat.

Watching the commercials, we note
the speed of the assault, messages
addressed to envy and ego.
We toast each other, high-heeled monsters,
and no country we can name.

'What is good and bad taste is very subjective,'
an ITV executive explains,
of ads shown during a play about women in Auschwitz.
'Of course we ruled out several categories
immediately – no food or vitamins,
hair preparations, holiday camps,
or gas products of any kind.'

His smile oils the screen.

Clawing at the pillows and the heaped
quilts, *high time,* I say, that the
dragon took hands with the pale princess –
shadow victim defended (sometimes) by
men and lances and smiling
back, always smiling –
first strike in a
quest selfish and long
negative to positive
(I never knew her name)

Take eat speak act

(the spiral deep in the storm,
the world turning over)

Judith Kazantzis

THE FRIGHTENED FLIER GOES NORTH (113)

She shakes in the take-off lounge.
Please stop the milk till further notice.
She buys a gin and tonic.
Please no papers till I let you know.
She buys a gin and tonic.
Goodbye my dear friends.

They are calling at the gate.
Her ticket reads, Bergen, Norway:
the blackhaired raven,
the light green Hanseatic larch,
the soft coiled herring.
She has fingered Norway, as God
Adam, across the globe

from a secluded velvet armchair.
Now the bell dings
that dings for her.

She has a body of Valium and gin
and seats it in the belly
of the body of a DC9.
The seats are tangerine.
The hostesses wear blue.

The DC9 begins to pant,
flicker, sweat and trot forward.
Suddenly she is assumed upwards.

The firmament rolls like an eye.
The speck dances on the glistening cornea.
The startled open sky bowls each side
down to its violet lids.
She covers her face.

You are a little worried.
The captain himself,
Captain Willemsen,
bids me bid you welcome. Come!

She sways in the cockpit behind him.
He is blonde, he is fifty-one.
He masters, with a checklist,
two hundred switches.
The air is squared with voices
and his is one.
The ordinariness!
he tells her: see, we're
on the job,
effect follows cause, cause
may be grasped, effect
obtained; to sum up,
speed versus drag.
Slats, flaps, height, knots,

wind, radar, coffee,
spoilers, also ailerons.

He turns a thumbnail knob,
the speck ascends the towering eye,
ailerons, coffee, the coast
emerald on radar,
diamond to her wonder.

Willemsen, the blonde captain of fifty-one
spreads for her the piebald ranges,
the flower-blue shuttered sea, the myriad rocks.
The nosecap wheel roars, the
white practical way untucks
on the green promontory,
Balancing, trembling,
a fly on the pin of physics
unhurt,
the assaults, unfelt, the opposing airs,
the howls and groans, the lamentations.
To tread floods
unseen, save in a quiver on scales,
a tremble of needles.

You see after all – says
fiftyish Willemsen
(as they set down,
like a fast pony trap,
ailerons, spoilers, woa),
you feel soothed, no? it
is ordinary,
he says to the frightened flier.

But she walks to the gate
of Bergen, that a finger
touched in London,
with her gin pink wind pink cheeks
and her high altitudinous feet,
ready and ravenous

for the opened sandwich,
the rush of the ravens of Odin,
and rich
with the cancellation of newspapers,
the stopping of milk.

Christina Jenkins

(114) SUNDAY MORNING

So warm I may melt.
So wonderful a room; hoards of turquoise threads, oak
caress.
My mother's wedded cooking sings in wrapping paper tune,
The carpet screams, shredded victoriously by the cat –
A glorious ginger dripping sunlight, erotic glides, glarny
eyes.

Reading James Joyce; red cover warm as blood covered
nightmares,
Heavy as lead.
Smoke, winter blue haze, stirs in a cheap china teacup,
I swallow it up, throat as hot as hell.
Scattered wedding photographs, or my frozen childish
sugar grin,
Visions of a birthday party friend.

My father with his newspaper face,
Around which long pink fingers curl. Once his little girl –
Best Sunday dress, silly giggles, then.
The cat rejects my hug, his plate of wet globular meat
rivals me,
A canned treat, companion of bone white dagger teeth.
It disappears down the rose pink raw wetness of his throat.
Squelching end.

The rain hammers a new world beyond the soul-sister-
window
Pane of family cottage cake life.
Colour television dreams, roast beef, snoozy scenes.
Born to this, for sixteen years mine.
Face scrubbed so clean, so bright. (Are cats really colour
blind?)
'An 'A' level student', Sunday morning ink fights.

Phone rings. It's not for me.
My mother's voice seeps through the council blue wood,
Middle-aged giggles,
Fluff.
Reading on – the aura of Cuban rum, far away; sad smiles.
My Dad's soft bed linen eyelids are closed, head gently
bent in sleep.
Mum's Sunday dinner sighs pinch the air. The cat's curled.
Only for me Sunday morning is not routine. I dream.
Only I have enough insolence for that.

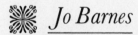

Jo Barnes

CLINIC DAY (115)

Her thin puny little body,
contorted in rage and indignation.
As I placed her in the cold white scoop,
Of the plastic scales.
The self-satisfied clinic mothers,
dangled their fat, round faced,
pink cheeked little monsters.
And gleefully compared notes.
'My little Wayne is taking eight ounces of his feed.'
'He has all his milk teeth has our Arnold.'
'John can count backwards in Urdu.'

I retrieved my scarlet-faced, toothless, wailing banshee.
'How many ounces does she take of her feed,'
enquired Mrs. Neat as a new pin.
'I'm not sure, she's breast fed,' I apologised.
A withering look of distaste followed by,
'Oh I always like to see EXACTLY,
how much Nigel is taking.'
Exit inferior mother,
with squalling inferior infant.
Social Worker 'Isn't she walking yet at 15 months?'
'Er no, I'm afraid not.'
'Perhaps if you had all carpet, in the hall and dining room,
she wouldn't be afraid of falling.'
Em tucked one leg under her,
in a sitting position,
and scooted crab-like across the room,
in a defiant gesture, that's my girl!

Maureen Burge

(116) THE DIET

Sat in the pub
Drink flowing free
Everyone's merry
Cept poor old me
I'm starving

I have to sit
in the corner
All quiet
The trouble you see
I'm on a diet
I'm starving

No whisky, no gin
Why did I come in
no ploughman's lunch
like that greedy bunch
I'm starving

Shall I walk to the bar
I won't go too far
Just a pkt of crisps
and one drink
I'm starving

Then I think I'll have
when I've finished this fag
some chicken and chips
in a basket
I'm starving

No I can't keep quiet
I'll shout, Bugger the diet
I'm absolutely starving

Pat Arrowsmith

POLITICAL ACTIVIST LIVING ALONE (117)

I'm middle-aged,
a child;
live in a toy shop,
pub;
shall never stop
enjoying my mobile,
glass animals,
shot of rum,
disco lamp.

Life is so dun
drear
dread –
to have fun
at all
you need the odd drink
and shimmering thing.

Picketing;
agitating;
working;
trudging
sunday by sunday
from marble arch
to whitehall,
embankment,
paddington

for the right to work,
free speech,
equality of race,
sex,
species,
sheer survival –
this vital cause
or that –

you need a bit of
glitter,
liquor,
colour,
warming

when you get back
to your empty flat . . .

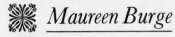

Maureen Burge

DISILLUSION (118)

Look at him, over there
Watch him turn his head and stare
I think he fancies me

See the way he turns around
See him look me up and down
I'm sure he fancies me

Look at his lovely jet black hair
I don't really like 'em fair
I just know he fancies me

He's coming over, aint he great
He's gonna ask me for a date
I knew he fancied me

Hang on just a minute though
He's heading straight for my
mate Flo
And I thought he fancied me

Tara Flo, I'll go on home
I spose I really should have known
He didn't fancy me

I don't like un anyway
He's ugly
I don't fancy he

Gillian E. Hanscombe

(119) *From* JEZEBEL: HER PROGRESS

23 Jesus People

Mrs Snatcher Thatcher
runs the land.
Her right hand knows
what her left hand wants.
She juggles with both hands
behind our backs.

She believes in sin.
The sin of the poor is their idleness;
the sin of the sick is their dependence;
the sin of the children is their ignorance;
the sin of the women is their helplessness;
the sin of the workers is their discontent.

Sweat and tears do not placate her.
She snatches back
what she says has not been earned
and juggles it abracadabra
into a missile
which she says will defend the
poor
sick
children and
women and
workers

against some greater evil than
poverty
illness
illiteracy
humiliation and
slavery.

Her charisma is built on that mystery.
What is that greater evil?

All the people wonder
and stare
and dare not disbelieve.

Mrs Snatcher Thatcher believes in sin.
She expunges evil
by creating missiles.

Janet Dubé

AUTOBIOGRAPHY (120)

When I first opened my eyes
everything appeared to be clean
and tidy; the sheets, the little
pillowslip, the trees
outside the window.

Later, I began to notice.
The underground shelter
was very dirty, and when
bombs fell, they left
a lot of rubble;

but I kept busy.
Only when they stopped
me working did
the dirt begin to stick.

I kept my eyes shut,
but after some years
it appeared that this
was no longer permitted.

I opened them wide:
not permitted either.

I am learning to live
in the half light.
It makes the dirt
more natural, somehow.

Even here in the convent
there are droppings,

blood sweat and tears.
They haven't given back
my work, till all the perfumes
of Arabia would not sweeten
this hand.

(121) SO TO TELL THE TRUTH

so to tell the truth
we must make fiction

but who is bold enough
to tell the truth,
two legged stranger?

on this narrow margin
between your world and mine
much has been said:

we have gone backwards
and forwards, crossing
and recrossing, passing

I cannot say what,
something hidden,
that neither your

language nor mine
has words to tell:
let be let be

follow the plants
answer the sun
follow the moon:

the secret is between,
together, crossing,
passing, noticing

this and that; nonsense,
beauty; our children;
your silvery voice;

my silvery tail

Pat Arrowsmith

CHRISTMAS STORY (1980) (122)

Christmas, season of streamers, coloured lights;
occasion of sorrow, pain for many
recollecting bygone times:
childhood's merry celebration;
joy with their own family.

But remember, many carols warn
the sleeping infant will awake
to extreme agony and loss,
torture, death upon the cross.

That child was born on Christmas Day
(so many people say)
to bring hope, happiness and peace;
not mourning, nostalgia, grief.

Yet Christmas was a hardship saga:
the parents obeying colonial law
went to be censused, over-taxed;
suddenly found that they were homeless;
the mother's labour pains endured
in a filthy, stinking stable;
his first cot, infested manger;
first visitors, a group of peasants
bemused by mass hallucination;
his later ones, regal astrologers
who, having seen a flying saucer
or disintegrating meteor,
arrived equipped with costly presents,
gradiose, useless, foreboding,
who, all unwitting, on their journey
launched genocide of Jewish babies
by a jealous, ruthless puppet king.

So Jesus with his parents fled;
trudged wearily across the desert;
found that they were refugees
in an unknown foreign land.

Yet still we celebrate that sad day
(which was probably in February),
treat it as a greedy feast,
over-eating, over-drinking,
slaughtering people on the streets.

And still the poor are homeless, taxed,
censused, computerized;
Jews are cursed, abused, attacked;
dissidents kidnapped, tortured, killed;
people flee from cruel dictators,
become unwelcome refugees;
deadly satellites explode
astoundingly in midnight skies.

So can it be a Prince of Peace
was really born one winter's night
in the Rome-ruled Middle East?
What of the torture, murders, war
perpetrated in his name
from that first Christmas Day to this?
How can you possibly explain
that wicked or misguided men
will fire rockets to destroy the world
he came that Christmas Day to save?

Astra

BLOODY PAUSE (123)

this menopause of mine
pauses too frequently
to render me much service:
i want my bloodletting to be gone
after three decades of woman's potency

my cycles are sufficient now
just as they are:
my womb is seasoned
my tubes tied
my ovum spent
my cervix settling down for better things

yet still i bleed from time to time –
only smears and stains
but still escorted by pains and aches
before the blood begins and even afterwards:
my pace slackens
my stomach swells
my shoulders stiffen
my eyelids shut

mistakenly i had assumed
my clockwork periods
had come full circle –
that i could pacify the goddess otherwise –
with poetry perhaps –
so i shall offer up this bloody piece to her

and pause a while

Judith Kazantzis

(124) A WOMAN MAKING ADVANCES PUBLICLY

A woman making advances publicly
twin spots of rouge
her chin quivers
yeast mask she took
for freshness, and forgot
to wipe off, before the door.
So gay her brave
eyes and the whites, like a dog,
upturned;
twin rouge, she's bright gaunt
thirty-nine, like me.
Where from this crow, dredged
up so, this whore, to scare?
Times lost, of the bright lined smiles,
the timid skull
X-rayed straight out.
Where from, my father,
learned and rapt father,
when, knee high to a grasshopper
I stood by your leg
you on the lawn bench, long
time past, reading
a holy book,

I standing in my best dress
shy into my mother's camera.
I did not look so strange.

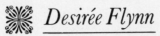

Desirée Flynn

FROM THE RAIN FOREST (125)

I

Soon I will climb the hill to the sunlight,
from under the secret vines.

Soon.

But now seem rooted in the scented leaves,
in the years of leaves, in the soft shadows
where mountain ash and turpentine are talling to the sky.

For this is how it is, the last parting,
now the last of my children is grown and gone,
and the warm firelit circle is broken beneath the trees.

Time ran a flash flood that rolled a creek to a river.
Unbelieving, I stood on one side: they stood on the other.

They waved, and ran fast to their gold-bright horizons;
on their shimmering plain they grew small and far.

It is dark here under the tree ferns.

II

The track is slippery, where water drips,
and narrow, to drop down a thousand feet,
so watch your step, being no longer young;
you could fall back to the gorge you're climbing from.

You can work your way up, if you take it slowly.
Stop

where a sudden flower leaps outward from a ledge
to snatch the mind with brilliance

or, equally, illuminate with gentleness.

You're treading aromatic heath, rough ground,
you've reached the top.

III

Catch your breath in the wind, where the mountains
watch from the westward.
Rejoice in the hard wind under the bare sun.

IV

Self expands to take in hawk take in hawk's gulf of air
self is rhythm pattern flight self fills up the sky
stretched thin to transparency to reflected light

V

contracting
to time
contracting
in time
disjoining
reforming
point atom unit
entity

VI

being un-rigid conduit for
whatever is of purpose or design
the catalyst of changing and becoming
coming towards wholeness towards singleness

Naomi Replansky

I MET MY SOLITUDE

(126)

I met my Solitude. We two stood glaring.
Truly I trembled to meet him face to face.
Then he saying, and I with bent head hearing:
'You sent me forth to exile and disgrace,

'Most faithful of your friends, then most forsaken,
Forgotten in breast, in bath, in books, in bed.
To someone else you gave the gifts I gave you,
And you embraced another in my stead.

'Though we meet now, it is not of your choosing.
I am not fooled, and I do not forgive.
I am less kind, but did you treat me kindly?
In armored peace from now on let us live.'

So did my poor hurt Solitude accuse me.
Little was left of good between us two.
And I drew back: 'How can we stay together,
You jealous of me, and I laid waste by you?

'By you, who used to be my good provider,
My secret nourisher, and mine alone.
The strength you gave me I must use against you
And now with all my strength I wish you gone.'

Then he, my enemy, and still my angel,
Said in that harsh voice that once was sweet:
'I will come back, and every time less handsome,
And I will look like Death when last we meet.'

Asphodel

(127) ON THE PILGRIM'S WAY IN KENT,
AS IT LEADS TO THE COLDRUM STONES

Breaking the morning ice on the well's bucket was no great hardship
Or carrying the water through the snow to the house
That had withstood four hundred years, and perhaps before
Had been a pointer, a shelter, even a hospice
For those going further,

Along the hard track, there on the hill's breast, aligned with the markers
That led to the stone circle and the sacred trees.

They had walked along the way then long before
As I walked; broke the ice, warmed it for drinking
Bending against the East wind pouring down over the woodland,
Massing up snow thigh deep; but we all could push through it,

The Way's magic pulled us through it, winter and summer.

There was no defeat by the weather there; suddenly
Poppies danced out in the sunlight against green verges
Burning out under a skylark's exaltations
While the delicate scabious curtsied, and the huge white daisies nodded,

And small lizards darted as they heard a footstep;

While I walked the Way each day and then again each day
Coming to the stillness from the bypass and the traffic
I watched the leaves grow, and blow;

As they had done before; and climbed the hill to the dewpond or walked the
lane to the water that never would drain away

On the way to the stones in their circles and the notch in
the ridge of hills.

They say the people had lived there after the Ice Age.
We broke the ice together to keep on living.

And if I die tomorrow, will I be gone?

Desirée Flynn

THE COLLECTOR (128)

At sixty, it might be well to start
a collection of intangible photographs.
Take a headful of transparencies, perhaps,
to hold up behind your eyes in a small room,
or project upon the weary, shiny walls
that could be there, already, waiting.

Take wide sweeping frames, a painter's canvas:
horizons that dissolve in blue and blue;
a sea of grass, a sea of sand; take oceans.
Then use your eyes as telephoto lens
to catch the black hilarity of leech,
tree-hopper hopping blithely on his trees.

grey stone drips silver
rain and leaves
silver rain silver leaves
parrot lightning through the trees
gum blossom drift
is cloud is mist
two dissolving are one
'I live I live'
murmurs stone

If time does close you into that small room,
it might hold compensations, shutting out

from your soft chair or bed, from your soft conscience,
the helpless living and the hunger dead.
The little evils too; boredom of red
brick; a devil's tattoo of noise; caged birds.

Better not to watch tin-god-in-the-box
flick its bright violence. Project your slides:
inhale the essence of bittersweet sun scent,
of honey, the hot breathing of the bush;
let hands remember tree shape, rub rough bark,
Hear again the spirit sound of silence.

Diana Scott

(129) WINTER SOLSTICE POEM

Quiet now, feel the kindly pressure of darkness:
be aware of this.
In the warm room the candles are extinguished.
Beyond the window
iron ground rejects the snow
ice wind bears upwards.
Outside in the hall
celebrants are waiting.

It is the year's midnight: the shortest day.
On that magical threshold
the two eyes of the turning year
the frozen moon and the sun
standing one month in the summer sky
rise together
and the midwinter queen comes
to tell you that darkness
in due time, always becomes light:

You have chosen for the threshold of your home,
your heart, the lady of light

to give you this reminder;
you have crowned her with candles
dressed her in a white dress
Let people walk after her:
It is always done
In ordinary clothes
carrying red ribbons and tapers:
placed in her hands green branches
it is always done

and now in your darkened room
breathe in the darkness.
the candles are extinguished.
the table is adorned with pine horses, roses
and little trees, and you are waiting –
suddenly beyond the turn of the door
a moving radiance:
suddenly through the fear of the heart
comes the singing:
and all the while on iron ground
the short ordinary day is dying.

She is coming into your room: Lucia
She is coming, bearing green branches
Lady of the midwinter light.
She is there in your room, distant,
crowned with candles, singing a high song,
and the people are all looking at you kindly
and giving you presents
so you know that the day has come
though not for you, and you know that
as each year turns it will return,
though not for you, and you know
that the lady of light is lovely and returns
regardless, uncaring, like the grass.

Naomi Replansky

(130) IN THE SEA OF TEARS

Tentacled for food,
You range your underwater neighbourhood.

To look, to like, to eat, to break your fast!
Before you move an inch an hour is past.

Your prey is past, a swarm of scales, an eye,
A round fish eye, a rude unblinking eye.

You close on nothing. Slowly you untwine
Your many arms and trail them through the brine.

Now sailors at the surface hear you cry
And from those heights they cannot fathom why.

For there are agile creatures all around
Who dart like flames through this rich hunting-ground,

And others who lie still and gaping wide
And make no move; but armies come inside.

Diana Scott

(131) PRAYER FOR THE LITTLE DAUGHTER
BETWEEN DEATH AND BURIAL

Now you are standing face to face with the clear light
believe in it
Now you have gone back into where air comes from
hold fast to it
Now you have climbed to the top of the topless tower
and there are no stairs down
and the only way is flight past the edge of the world
do not remember us

Like the new moon in the sky of the shortest day
you came to us
as the candles burnt with a steady light behind misty
  windows
you whispered to us
as the singers moved behind doors of un-attainable rooms
you burst in on us
Lady of the shortest day, silent upon the threshold
carrying green branches

Lady of the crown of light going into clear light
be safe on your journey
Bright lady of the dark day, who pushed back the darkness
say nothing to us
as we plod through the frozen field
going from somewhere to somewhere
do not speak to us
as we stand at the centre of the frozen lake
and trees of cloud stand over us
forget us

When we come to you we shall find you
who have seen Persephone
you whom our mothers called Lady of the city
will welcome us with tapers, and believe in us
When small harsh birds bubble and pump in our nude trees
and water will rush and gush through the slippery street
and two skies will look at each other
one of air and one below
of water
you will rest with us, and of us:
Lady of the shortest day
watch over our daughter
whom we commit to the grass

Asphodel

(132) WINTER SOLSTICE – FOR FRANK

Your turn came, and you chose to take it,
You chose to go, to be the chosen one.
You chose to move along the tiered doorways,
Through the narrow walls of the rough tunnel
Through the flashing fires;
You chose to eat the berry, to savour the leaf;
To swim out into Lethe and plummet downwards.
You chose to take your turn, to push out through the
swing doors into nowhere, or redemption.
You said: seventy years are enough.
(I still say, they are not enough).

But it was your time. You had borne pain,
Loneliness of the knowledge of the approach of death.
Someone has to go, to leave the circle;
You let it be you.

If we dance round the candles, I remember you;
If I pick up new light and look up for new light
I remember you;
If you hold the passage, the tunnel, the curtains across the
door
Away from me; giving me more time in the light;
If you guard the entrance against me,
Unroll a carpet of time for me
In the light,

One time the shadows must tire for you
You will choose at last to move inwards
You will let the curtain drop.

And will expect me one day.

Judith Kazantzis

IN MEMORY, 1978 (133)

I want to lament the princess who was killed,
gunned down by the henchmen of her grandfather,
in the main square of Jeddah;
she was a princess so she was gunned,
ordinary women are stoned to death for adultery,
their lovers lose their heads, which is to
teach other men not to;
for the women the lorry reverses into the square,
tips out a pile of ordinary stones
which at sunset are picked out by the faithful
under the adjuration of a holy man;
they being all men; the adulteress is made to
stand upright inside a sack,
they throw the stones at her till the sack falls
over, and go on till she dies.

When the sun sets, here the crescent
rises – she sees neither,
having been a believer all her life, done
everything dutifully but one thing:
which was to remain behind her black seven veils
every living moment: to
take her flesh to sackcloth from birth
to death; to
keep their eyes clean
for God, and his rigid kings and small fathers
on earth
she salaams down
on to, dear God, well trodden ground.

Harriet Rose

(134) MELLISANDRA

They looked at me all ghosts
and silent observers
who observe only second hand
recording day to day trivia
like symptoms of some minor illness.

What I have seen would only shock them lightly
in the manner of lewd gossip. Lewd gossip
when my child among rows of naked and already dead
was paraded along in the snow. Why hadn't they selected
me for death?

My face belies me.
I had expected to age rapidly in the war years.
But I am always the same, just thinner.

In the camp masks of ice drip off slowly.
My face, on the contrary hardened.
But my soul squeezed through.
They were unable to squeeze it out.
And at moments of illumination
it shines through my face.
Of my face they have made an art.

Monsters and saints grow by the same process
out of the hulks of the human frame.
And there is rain enough to drown the world in.

Back then my fingers were icicles always growing longer
constantly longer like an upward creeper.
I had three children and Victor who was never taken
fighting in a foreign army.

Victor and I had some sort of childhood together
before he began to grow bitter.
Now, even, he holds me in his great strength
and whispers things out of B pictures in various languages

as we have lost our own
while we are roofed by the rain shimmering
and these women who were safe always
whisper gossip and grow restless because they can't marry.
Then they come and offer their help.

Victor spits out words as though he would choke on them.
Once we had three children and a house with a white wood
fence
a dog barking in the hedge – barking. How the guard dog
growled.
And when I complete my ritual of dying complete in its
beauty
and offer myself like a prayer he will curse God.
The weaker I grow the more luminous the more
he loves me with his soul. Cannot strength be beautiful
like the lithe cat tumbling among tree branches?
These women parade in and out like a chorus of nuns of
ghosts
needing our blood for their gossip preparing the ritual
supper.
My name was Mellisandra which flowed once from his lips
like laughter
and now seems unsuitable.

Lorna Mitchell

THE HERMAPHRODITE'S SONG (135)

Don't touch me
Don't touch me
I am
The hermit celibate bone with no marrow
Hanging like a hook from my shoulder.
Bitter sharp pain unreal
Teeth skull and finger nail

Pinned to the wall
Watching you crawl
Squirm ooze everywhere
You slug slime swamp
You creeping cornucopia
Don't come near me, leave me alone
I am the picked-clean dry desert bone
Let the sand trickle through my hollow back
Ah! let the sun burn my mouth and lips black
And the desert dry my eyes in horizon.
When you smile your face drips slowly waxily
I shall wipe your fatty buttery melting mucus
From my pure white brittle vertebrae
When you speak you smell
With the food you gorge
Don't put your pudgy fingers near your breasts
And squirt your milk at me.
Let me out
Let me out
Don't come near
Don't come near
You don't know who I am,
My vagina is a chalky cave
My penis and testicles I gave
To the worms
I am above the earth and far beyond
My mind is a supernova diamond
The crystals are infinite in number time and space
You try to drag me down in your morass
You try to seep your earth into my pores
You will try to bring your tidal wave onto my shore
Engulfing me with algae, coelenterates and diatoms.
You are the earth, you are the sea
I am the stratosphere
I am the purest gases above the highest mountain
You are murky depth beneath the deepest ocean
You are flesh flesh

I am spirit spirit
Noli me tangere
Noli me tangere
Noli me tangere

(INSTRUMENTAL BREAK)

They took away my body and put it in a box
They flung it in the ocean and it came up on the rocks
There were mountains to the north
Sandy beaches to the west
The sun came up and lit the water
And a tern swooped on its nest
Someone came down to the shore
Collecting driftwood for her fire
She saw the box and clambered over
And she tried to prize it open
Something stirred inside the coffin
Fingers moved toes stretched head swivelled
The lid creaked the lock bent I struggled
I burst through I opened my eyes
I heard the waves I saw the towering skies
A frightened woman gazed at me
But she didn't go away
I longed for
          grass sap sea spray gull cry
          rainfall windlift and life
And I whispered
Touch me
Kind tender woman touch me
Touch me
And she leaned across
And gently
And she gently gently gently
Touched my cheek.

Stephanie Markman

(136) *From* THE RIME OF THE ANCIENT FEMINIST*

VII

They lived out in a women's house
which stood beside the shore.
I'd seen them at a meeting when
they'd said they couldn't work with men
and slammed right out the door.

They'd asked the other women there
to talk about their lives,
to speak of their experience
as daughters, mothers, wives.

I'd held back then I held back now
afraid of giving way,
still fearing if I gave myself
I'd give myself away.

Still standing rigid, speechless, frigid,
staring all about,
until I felt the room go swimming,
heard a woman shout:
'For god's sake get some air in here:
I think she's passing out.

'This place is really claustrophobic,
that's what's made her sick.
The window's locked, or blocked, or jammed;
let's try to get it open, and
let's get her outside, quick.'

'You're always rushing into things,'
another woman said.
'I'd always go,' the first said, slow,
'where angels fear to tread.'

Then, with a grin, 'If fools rush in,
I'll gladly play the fool.'

They laughing took me by the arm
and took me through the hall

Across the bar I stumbled on,
with one on either side.
The door clanged shut behind my back,
I found myself outside.

I almost turned and rushed back in,
in momentary fright,
in gazing at the blazing moon,
the stark black, dark black night.
But firm and calm they kept my arm
and kept me to my flight.

My panic ebbed away away;
the women onwards urged.
Their energy surrounded me
and through my body surged
a wave of pleasure, sweet and strong:
I stopped, I gave a moan.
I gently shook their hands from me;
and stood there on my own.

Then from the sand, there blew inland
a wind, both soft and light.
I smelt the salt smell of the sea,
and smelt it with delight
and took a mighty breath of it
and ran with all my might.

And now I stood beside the sea,
the salt tears on my cheek.
The women came and called my name,
as if to bid me speak.

The sea was washing, washing in;
beneath the moon it stirred.
I turned to share my life with them;
they took it in, they heard.

I poured it out, the pain, the doubt;
I ripped away the shell.
When I was bare before their stare,
they spoke of theirs as well.

Since then, there have been moments when
I feel it all again,
and feel compelled to speak, to tell,
to spell out all my pain.

I go to every women's centre,
every woman's place:
I look into the women's eyes,
and now and then I recognise
a certain look, a face.

The women come, now one by one
they trickle through the door.
But deep within, I hear a din,
a dim and muted roar.
The sound of women's fighting hits me,
splits me to the core.

Oh sister, I have lived too long
in barren, arid lands;
a dismal place, without embrace,
without the touch of hands.

I've seen too much dissension,
too much strife, too much despair;
and still I wait to celebrate
the sisterhood we share.

To know again that all my pain
is not confined to me;
that other women share the hurt,
that though our lives take root in dirt
we still grow strong and free.

This one more thing I'll tell you, sister,
then I have to go;
if anger is our weapon, then
be careful where you throw.

If anger is our weapon
don't ignite it showing off.
For anger is explosive, and
right now it's going off.

The woman watched her walk away,
how slow and sure she strode;
and thus, without a backward glance,
she went off up the road

and left the woman sitting there
to meditate at leisure,
to wait until her friends came through
and hug them all with pleasure.

*** The Ancient Feminist has moved from marriage, via deep anger and confusion, to male dominated radical politics. Finally, taking refuge in the toilets from a meeting, she encounters women-identified women.**

Harriet Rose

THE WEDDING COAT (137)

He calls you in his wedding coat
whiter than wind on the roof that coat
the air smelling of midsummer
calling that girl whose name is Mellisandra

Earth all wed out of body
is the grave cloth of some higher principle.
A badly played blues number haunts the wind.
In summer – shade is Negro.

And for Mellisandra
that stick of a girl
he romanticized as vulnerable.
'Why do men like thin girls?' she had asked
'because they think they can beat them up.'
And then she fell into her own trap
of making her name lyrical
like the hair's breath kiss
that caught her in the new wine of midsummer
drowning in it fly tossed.

His voice was rich and deep and stark
like the jazz trumpet in a wedding march
isolating the more striking images
in order to tame and wife them
with his blood. Paper flowers
shot through his breath
notes of song hiss like steam irons
women have names like flowers exotic flowers.

Names were important as omens
names became omens.
She had flung her soul from some wider island
and loss of memory made tears.

Mellisandra, Mellisandra the limp air holds you.
It is damper and forlorn as sweat in his bulging waistband.
Mellisandra the air will grip you tight as a metal band
that ring to have and hold but you can't hold it.
There is nothing to hold onto not husband
not the nettled grass or the old lady
who accuses you of being someone else
not the words to name things.

Look at Mellisandra as she dances in the shadows
as she shrinks into the shadows
trying to grow weightless into pavement shrink into the
pavement

as she shrinks into her lover's arms love making much of
the repetition.

His wedding coat hangs from the ceiling like a limp bulb.
It is the mute partner of her waltz.

Anon.

POEM FOR JACQUELINE HILL (138)

This woman is getting on her last bus
She is paying her last fare
for her the number one, green and cream, Leeds double
decker
moves up the dark roads of the killing city
Her number is up;
For her it's the last time that
bracing her body against the sway of the bus in motion
she moves up to choose her last seat
in the ordinary November evening of her last ordinary day
This woman is about to die – you know, you'll read it in
the papers
the next day, and the next day, and the day after that –
wearing, the police told us, when she died, a grey duffle
coat with
brown overcheck, blue jeans, brown shoes, a white scarf
spectacles, and Fair Isle patterned mittens – and you –
the other women –
know now, that she died
and you know that she was wearing all that
but perhaps it is not quite bearable to think
that before the newspapers, the police
the slow stain of fear spreading like a cloud through the
guilty city

there was a moment like any other between nine and ten
  in the evening
when she had not yet died
(and the bus is still moving)
and we were all doing something quite ordinary
(and the bus is slowing down now)
and Jacqueline Hill, now the thirteenth member of the
Ripped-up dead,
was alive, ordinary, admirable, easy to like, tired,
was about to die, and we did not know, and we did
  nothing
there was a moment when
(and she is stepping off the bus)
And I keep seeing her, the gesture endlessly repeated,
  getting off the bus
It could have been any one of us – the short walk home
ending in no home, no warmth, no light, only the man
  with the hammer
smashing into the skull, and the sharp piercing instruments:
crossing the dark streets all this autumn I have seen
the shadowy fall of the hammer on my own head
and yet I too was silent, did nothing, and the moment was
  his own
and quiet in the lamplight
this woman is getting off her last bus.

* * *

Now, stealing fearful or chaperoned through the shadowed
  streets –
night, in Leeds, in November, is *fifteen hours long*
We know only, that each man, or group of men on these
  streets

is an enemy, or if not the enemy waiting for us,
not our *personal* enemy, then one walking at large,
unshadowed, free
while we, the survivors
pinned down under artificial light in our fragile homes
feel the pressure of dread in the darkness nudging the
panes,
thin as our skin – and hear the voices:
'No woman is safe' (It is the police this time)
'No woman should go out after dark – ' then in a whisper:
'but we men can.'
The voices ride in on the wind
that butts against the walls –
(walls vulnerable as our skulls) –
'No woman is safe' –
The voices climb in as draughts through the cracks –
'Women' – (it is all men speaking now)
'fear the dark, stay at home,
we cannot answer for the consequences
if you get on buses;
leave *us* the hunting paths in the city jungle –
be good: be stupid: never, never be free.'
And we remember
the woman, who was, or could have been,
our sister, student, colleague, friend, neighbour
ordinary, admirable, easy to like, tired
who got off a bus, and for whom there was no going home
and we, we the women who as yet survive, we say:
'We have waited a long time for anger,
but we are angry now
for each and every betrayal of trust
for each and every degradation, the greater and the less

for each and every evil done to women
– and all are remembered; and all are written down –
we are coming to claim our justice
that is justice for us all
for our blood cries out, and unnumbered women cry out
through our voices, and our time has come, and *we are coming*
yes, *we are coming.'*

* * *

(*A Curse for the Ripper: we turn your hatred back at you*)
We call on the dark power of women
to call down this curse on you who hate us: Ripper!
you who would extinguish us in blood:
we turn your hatred back at you
we turn your hatred back at you
Let your own hatred spell out the curse on you
May no roof shelter you
May no friend cheer you
May no water refresh you
May no beauty gladden your eyes
May your strength fail you
May you never, never go home
You would extinguish us in blood
but we mark you with our blood, Ripper, we mark you with our blood
We mark you with our blood, all you who rip and beat and tear
our bones, our flesh, our lives, our sisters' lives
our own lives, yes our precious lives
We mark you with our blood, Ripper, we mark you

with the blood of all of them, Ripper
yes all
And
The dark is growing for you
The fear is growing for you
and the blood of all of them, all thirteen, is upon you
and the curse of all of them, all thirteen, is around you
and the shadows are gathering for you
thirteen
thirteen long shadows
and there will be no evading them, no
not even in the last days
May they draw the light from your eyes, Ripper
May they draw the blood from your body, Ripper
till all you are is in the deep shadow
of your own hatred for us, Ripper,
following you swift and pathless as a scream
and you will kill no more:
LET IT BE SO

* * *

We, the women still left, the survivors,
we name you, the victims, we speak of you with love;
gently
our fingers touch the reproductions of your photographs:
Wilma McCann
Joan Harrison
Emily Jackson
Irene Richardson
Patricia Atkinson
Jayne Macdonald

Jean Royle
Elena Rytka
Vera Millward
Yvonne Pearson
Josephine Whittaker
Barbara Leach and just a few days ago:
20 years old, a student woman, entering the probation service:
Jacqueline Hill:
Leaving shattered parents, a teenage brother and sister –
I would have given my life for her, said the sick father;
A part of us died, her mother added:
Jacqueline Hill.
It was a dark road he sent you down
dead before your time, shadow on the walls of the killing city,
you rushed away, our anger, our love, our grief
could not catch up with you
anger, love, grief – you turn it back to us
fight now, you say, fight back while you still have the time:
This is the city – the city kills;
This is mankind – and mankind kills:
Remember each night crossed without fear is a small victory –
and you send us your dreams:
Let me be (you say)
Let me live in peace
Let my life be alright
Helpful to others, useful, a good life
I thought that was enough, (you say) that I was alright
How could it be me?
But it was me and I walked down
the dark road; never forget that, in your righteous rage:
for me, the death in darkness: to you, now, a hard dawn.

Index of First Lines